A LABOUR OF LOVE

THE NEW MAKERS IN CONTEMPORARY DESIGN, PREVIEWING A FUTURE OF RESPONSIBLE PRODUCTION, CIRCULAR THINKING, ETHICAL PRACTICE AND ORGANIC AESTHETICS

Lidewij Edelkoort & Philip Fimmano

Lecturis

*Designer
Index on page
444*

People know they need to slow down the pace of overconsumption and overproduction; otherwise our planet will be lost. The creative world gains insight and invents systems where values shift and design plays an activist role, developing ideas about sharing between designer and the worker, designer and the underprivileged, designer and the amateur, designer and the designer... This new era gives hope for other ways of perceiving what is considered success, renown and profit. Here, capital is strictly human.

This social consciousness coincides with an important movement in philosophy, where each material is believed to be alive and able to emanate currents of energy, deserving the right to exist as in human rights and animal rights. The manufacturing of found, recycled and reinvented materials is testimony to this theory. The urge for matter is such that all focus is given to that particular part of the creative process, often imposing form instead of following it, since materials seem to become a living emotional element, communicating in an autonomous way, talking through tactility and attracting through energy. The open source sharing of knowledge and innovative manufacturing will become the key to a society taking care of both people and planet.

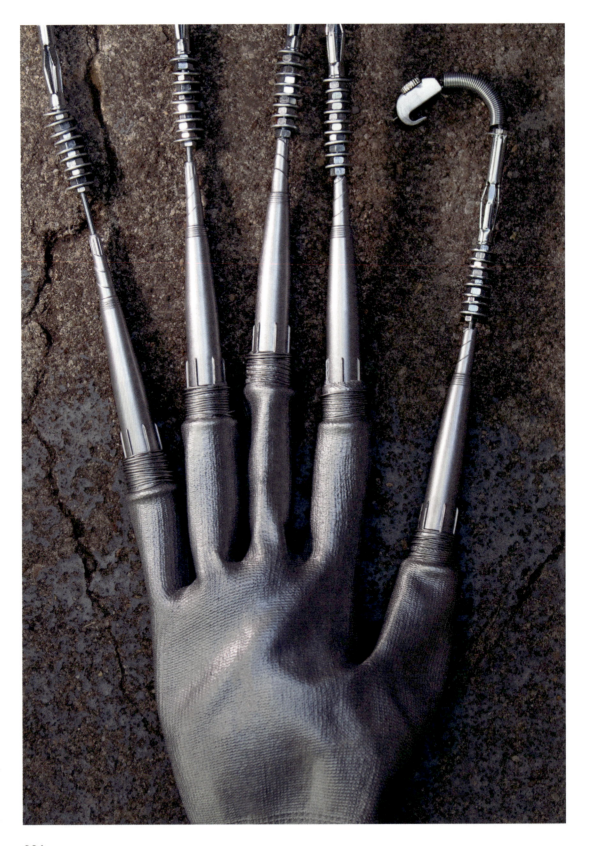

Since the beginning of the century, the design discipline has turned to the human hand as the antidote to a profound feeling of disarray, and the inability to cope with the superfluous industrial design of former decades. After a prolific arts & crafts period, we now observe that human hands want to once again espouse the machine, the printer and the loom – as if extending these hands like those of the famous Edward Scissorhands, prolonged tools that become playful and excited; intoxicating almost – and restlessly creative above all. Suddenly the hand and the machine work hand-in-hand to produce prodigious objects and materials that prepare us for a future to be created together and in collaboration.

A dedicated generation is leading this major movement, using machines to serve their purposes, reprogramming antiquated robots to construct their designs, hacking 3D printers to boost their forms and repurposing mechanical looms for contemporary creation. Suddenly the machine is no longer the antithesis of unbridled creativity but the handmaid of the designer; enabling, embellishing and advancing creative production. Man and machine finally merge and become one. Places for creating, sharing and manufacturing will become veritable cottage industries where the designer is at once the farmer, artisan and custodian of our earth, enamoured with all the phases and facets of the process. A labour of love.

– Lidewij Edelkoort & Philip Fimmano

In the history of design, the theory of social practice is an outsider principle that merits being better known and researched. For centuries the production of craft and food has governed human conditions and imposed social injustice, only interested in trade, gain and greed. Animals and people have become slaves to the process and are still living in dire circumstances that the world refuses to acknowledge. Plantations, mines, weaving mills and garment factories have cost many lives and tainted our cultural history with blood. Awareness is slowly growing, clarifying the facts of this scandalous past and present, to carefully start the processes of healing.

It was at the turn of last century that the arts & crafts movement was born, under the spiritual guidance of the designer William Morris who instigated a return to skilful and tasteful decorating, using nature as natural intelligence, mixing rigorous form with stylised embellishments. The movement advocated social reform and was anti-industrial to its core. Its makers professed the importance of local workshops, slower processes, better conditions and a policy of inclusion for all artisans.

It was not until the 1960s that another voice took up the debate to counteract the swinging economies of the times. Victor Papanek raised the issue of no longer tolerating design that doesn't account for the needs of people and the planet. He stated that designers need to be morally and socially responsible for the consequences their ideas have on society, including environmental impact.

At the start of the 21st century, another step was taken with the founding of a masters program called Man and Humanity at the Design Academy Eindhoven. The goal of the course was to explore design as an instrument of justice and inclusivity, using the gift of form to change the world and make it a better place. Victor Margolin writes that social design should not be considered charity but seen as a practice that is integrated in local economies, and that social design must be about the satisfaction of essential human needs versus the creation of products for market purposes only. Unfortunately, even today this philosophy sounds like a promise instead of reality.

CREATING COMMUNITY

The complexity of our current times has brought social design to the fore as a way to eradicate inequality and promote the inclusion of gender and race, to distribute work amongst the vulnerable and needy, and to set new rules for how to manage our dwindling resources and get rid of the waste in the world. New initiatives are designing systems to include workers in the creative process, and allow artisans to become artists in their own right. In a revival of the arts & crafts movement, workers collectives are again being built. De-colonializing and restructuring centuries-old production methods and hierarchies will yield new ideas for how to nourish the design discipline with holistic knowledge, illuminating the intuitive strength of the designer's mind and hand. Instead of designing products, creatives will be designing making systems, giving design back its initial strength of relating to and synthesizing our times.

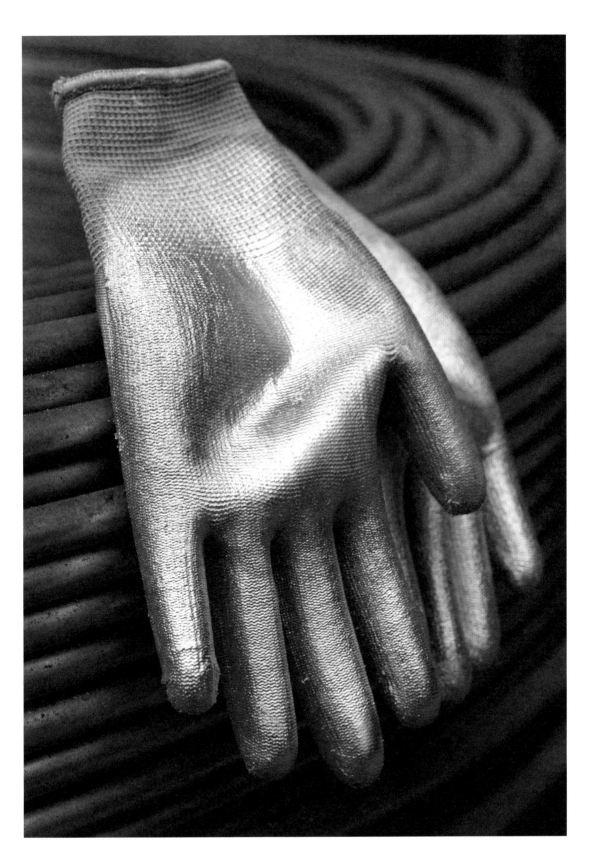

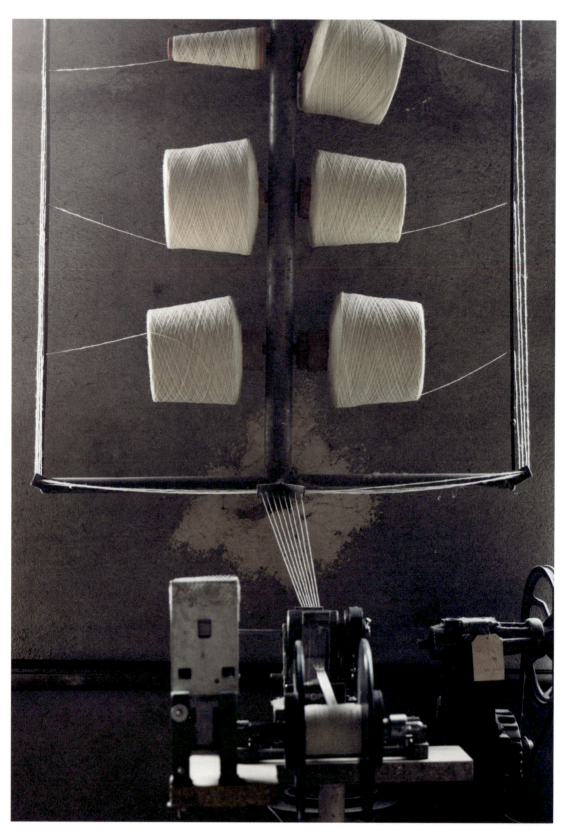

One peculiar question is if people learned weaving from the weaving bird or vice versa? The two species simultaneously developed the one up-and-down warp and weft technique as if in natural evolution. Textiles are almost as old as human civilization and have covered and embellished people since the Palaeolithic era. In the beginning it was nonwoven materials like bark, felt and fur that shielded people against the cold and rain. Later on they invented the coiling, braiding and spinning of grasses and animal fibres, while weaving techniques developed along the way. As early as the Bronze Age, women set up shop and created workshops where weavers produced yardages their husbands would take on the road to trade for other materials and livestock. After backstrap, frame and table looms, the machines became mechanical over the centuries, producing more regular materials. Weaving was considered a mathematical skill and the invention of the jacquard loom is therefore seen as the very first computer, creating intricate patterns woven for high-end interiors and fashion design. Textiles are made with multiple techniques such as the weaving of crossing threads, knotting macramé, knitting with two needles, braiding twisted threads and lace made from bobbing.

Derived from three domains, cloth can be made from the fibre of animals such as sheep and silk worms; from plants including hemp, cotton and linen; and from processing petroleum into synthetic yarns like nylon and polyester. The overpowering pollution of the textile industries has made synthetic qualities undesirable and companies with good practices are banning them. The recycling of waste is progressing with nylon reclaimed from fishnets, post-consumer polyester and plastics turned into fabrics. Spider silk, which is one of the strongest fibres on earth, is now developed as a biotech material, grown with water, yeast and sugar and the DNA of spiders – promising a future without synthetics. Recently, ancient fibres such as pineapple, bamboo, ramie and nettle have been rediscovered because of their qualities and the benefit of needing little water to be farmed.

WEAVING WONDER

Textile makers dedicate their lives to the crafting of exceptional cloth. The results are intriguing for the general public, making textiles totally relevant again. Running shoes made from jersey, raincoats from recycled nylon, sweaters knitted from rags; the research brings new ingredients such as milk proteins, kelp and crustaceans, with decayed flowers and food waste as dyeing agents. Laser cutting, pulp making and coiling are techniques that inspire new visions of fabrics. Most works use recycling as a key component, assembling leftovers from the manufacturing floor, collecting plastics from the oceans and using old clothes as new ingredients. The urge for textile making has become so strong that young people create design studios, work together as collectives and even start-up new textile mills. Cloth is no longer an endangered species; its revival is here and happening now.

Jeroen van Leur & Mae Engelgeer, textile panels, 2014

The pull of remnants from former societies is both of historic and contemporary importance. The collapse of human-made structures into a state of dilapidation is mostly due to natural disasters, terrorism and political skirmishes, or a decline in power and population, when previously prestigious vestiges become derelict due to long-time abandon, weathering and scavenging. Often the ruins are used as new building materials in the next period, thus in the Middle Ages, Roman ruins were used as quarries for opportunistic building projects, further damaging the original splendour. In the Renaissance, finding fallen fragments took on new meaning; admired and cherished for their innate beauty as venerated objects of decay and decadence, introducing a neo-classical mania and the birth of cultural awareness. In the Romantic period the odds and ends of castles, churches and temples became the subject of frenetic etchings, dark paintings and poetry readings, influencing garden follies, the decors of ruins and weathered waterfalls. The appeal of these remains has governed the history of art and design and influenced generations of aficionados to travel and explore, and therefore has become an important economy of collecting curiosities.

From the beginning of time, books recorded how magical remnants dominated inner cities and foreign regions, used in literature, architecture and design. Abstracting what is left from a richer heroic past speaks to the imagination and has made historical trends come back time and again. Thus the culture of ancient Egypt, the artefacts of pre-Columbian America, the teachings of ancient Greece as well as the legendary powers of Rome, keep on inspiring creative citations with the way these civilisations lived, celebrated, dressed and designed. The fragmented essence of remains keeps them alive, asking our brains to fill in the gaps and invent images and stories, demanding a stronger imagination and a deeper interest in the historical context. The decayed surfaces, discoloured murals and eroded stones are magical; a minimal presence with maximum impact, keeping culture and collectors intrigued.

ACCUMULATING REMNANTS

Design is again soul searching in the past, concerned by our recent overconsumption and overproduction which has ruined the process of making, eliminated the thrill of ownership and forever damaged the culture of beholding. Contemporary remnants today include giant floating plastic islands in the Atlantic, massive amounts of deadstock in the leather and textile industries, mountains of plastic bottles, kilometres of computer wires and overwhelming numbers of unsold garments and dumped objects. The design community decided to start better exploiting our remnants, accumulating them in a new creative vision of our times. Thus recycled plastics become our marble resins, recycled bottles our transparent fabrics, recycled garments our couture. Along the process of collecting these discarded ingredients, beautiful pieces are collaged together in multiple styles; a creative patchwork of hybrid design.

Misha Kahn, 2014

Without doubt, wood is the material that most sticks with us throughout life, from our baby crib to our burial coffin. It first becomes a rocking horse, a doll's house and an acoustic guitar. Then we grow up and need tables and cupboards, floors and beams, cabanas and houses. Wood also has a dominant role in art, used for sculptures, carvings, totems and blockprint making. And of course the multiple instruments humans have conceived since prehistoric times. Thus wood has had a great impact on human existence, from making music to playing house and providing culture.

Wood is the best known matter with which to shape objects, since it is porous and slightly malleable to begin with; carved into spoons and tools, built into furniture and bent into structural forms. This gifted material has been used since people began building shelters and boats, and over centuries its branches and logs have been burnt to give warmth to humans and their offspring. The organic material is composed of strong cellulose fibres that can be used for papermaking and textile weaving, maintaining generous fluidity in the fabrics. It is being studied as a material of the future; as a sustainable alternative to cellophane and acetate because of the fibre's silk-like aspects, and for further research in innovative cellulose yarns. There is a strong relationship between the properties of timber and the tree itself, since the density of wood varies by species and this is why designers carefully choose wood to sustain function and prolong a product's life. Wood is purchased for the long haul and is therefore literally ecological to the core. In an attempt to use fewer resources and recycle existing materials, engineered wood products are becoming a bigger part of the construction and packaging industries. Not only used for its structural assets but also as chips, sawdust and sprigs to make modest but beautiful plate materials. Since the beginning of this century, upcycled planks and floorboards have been popular and are positioned to continue in the future.

WORKING WOOD

Growth and harvest are in sync and in equilibrium for environmental purposes. As an abundant and carbon-neutral resource, wood has become a matter of choice and a source of renewable energy. Visible in the annual rings of the trunk and the patterns of knots that animate it, lumber is grown according to seasonal patterns and climatic conditions. These diverse properties are of interest for contemporary designers that rethink the uses of wood by including its flaws, showing its structural fragility as a beautiful accident in nature, to be cherished instead of hidden from the public eye. Wood today is made transparent, used for organic growth, chosen for its patterns and revered for its finishes. All the aspects of wood are gathered as aesthetic principles, including the reinvention of bark, the handwriting of twigs, a fascination with roots and the reintroduction of the log as an essential design reference.

Johannes Hermann, chair, 2013

From early times, humans used stone as weapons and tools, giving the name Stone Age to a period of more than three million years. This marked our prehistoric practice of hunting and gathering, improvising life from day to day, adjusting to the threat of war, and enjoying moments of celebration. Defence and desire existed side-by-side. The first humans used tools similar to the ones we have today, such as hand axes and weapons designed with an edge, a point, or a percussion surface. Carving locally-sourced fragments into rudimentary knives and hammers, moving larger pieces of rock to form dwellings and ritual places, bringing people together to profess their animistic faith. Found around the world, the dolman and other imposing monoliths served as monuments, sacred sites and icons of worship that reminded travellers of the overwhelming forces of nature, connecting heaven and earth. The mineral aspecs of stone were believed to have their own forces, as a living entity animated by its own molecular life and therefore pebbles were cherished and shaped to execute cutting, scraping and chopping tasks.

This bounty from the earth has gifted many generations of people with the most sturdy and reliable material to be used in building, in mechanical production systems such as milling and grinding and in components for industrial production at a later date. From the Tower of Babel to the Pyramids and the Pantheon, the heroic architecture of stone has been worshipped for its superhuman and godly presence. Only matched by the imposing Inca vestiges of the Americas.

Concerning the dynamic between rocks and humans, stones have kept on rolling when production systems had them build walls, cover roofs, design floors and beautify surfaces with the noblest of materials such as slate, granite and marble, which are still in use today, and actually making a comeback as an expensive form of natural wallpaper. Design and architecture remain attracted to these minerals and their lively abstract patterns. Whether random and natural or orchestrated and cultural, rocks are connected to the wealthy and therefore have an old school glamorous appeal.

CARVING STONE

Today designers no longer want to pillage the earth of its riches and try to find new ways of dealing with stone as a material for function and ornamentation. They listen to their conscience when expressing primitive form and archaic aesthetics, exploring the waste from the quarry and mining industries as raw materials. They set out to only use discarded boulders and smaller pieces of rock and marble to transform their instincts into animistic objects. Their carvings have an innate character, deserving of veneration as spiritual sources of design. Designers also invent stone-like surfaces by mixing minerals and other matter with lighter components like paper or textiles, and even plastic. They recreate stone and reconceive existing objects into new shapes. This resetting of the earth's materials will continue to thrive; a new Stone Age in the making?

Kueng Caputa, Too Hard to be True, 2013

Marjan van Aubel & James Shaw, Well Proven Chair, 2012

Just as human genius invented mashed foods, ground corn and pounded dough in different parts of the world, the idea of making pulp was as instinctive and universal. The shredding and smashing of leftover materials into new shape was born at the beginning of culture with the invention of paper and the idea of papier mâché, used for masks, dolls, boxes and mobile furniture. First ancient civilizations would use plant fibres such as papyrus to create pulped material when strips of bark were woven together, beaten into sheets and polished by hand. Pulp used in more modern making processes involves maceration, producing a much finer slurry of cellulose that is dried into a thinner material to work with. The goal of pulping is to break bulk material – be it in chips, stems or roots – combined with a polymer that binds the fibres together and gives longevity to the fragile matter; keeping the bulk from breaking.

Pulp is a way to create magic from poor materials and play games with modest means; since it is humble, fibrous and ultra lightweight, prepared by separating fibres from scrap wood, plant residues and paper waste, as well as textile rags. At first the pulp was made from bamboo, mulberry, sandalwood, straw and textiles like hemp, linen and cotton. From the late 13th century, the custom was to use discarded tattered clothing, fishing nets and fabric bags to create affordable raw material, hence the name of rag paper and the rag trade. Later on, the focus shifted to wood fibres and dust, turned into goo to give the material a second life.

PULPING SHAPE

Now in the 21st century, pulp has been rekindled and given new meaning with paper objects and furniture, cardboard offices and solid textile materials. The paste is reinvented by a young generation of designers, conscious of the abundant availability of discards and the problems trash culture has caused. The influx of fast fashion, fast food and fast products is overwhelming, and rescuing the planet has become a common call. Not only do they crush and mash and shred, they also sculpt and layer the macerated matter onto preconceived frames to hold their shape. The discipline is inventive and intuitively adds touches of tactility, defining raw finishes and including other elements like plastic and food refuse for tinting. As a movement, pulp is only just beginning; and will grow with our need to have inexpensive but durable ideas explored as the components of a sustainable future.

Paul Cocksedge, Excavation: Evicted, 2017

The study of the ancient is consecrated to the objects manufactured by humans, found through the excavation of fragments that narrate the customs and lifestyles of former civilisations. Uncovering the tools, spoons, potteries, clothes, dwellings, wall paintings and infrastructure laid bare how people travelled and settled, how they engaged in rituals and exchanges, how they made themselves beautiful with make-up and fragrance, and how they ate and cooked food; including using fruits, honey and herbs at an early stage to give taste to hunted meats and fish. Capable and independent nomadic women travelled vast distances, weaving their way to acquire income and gain respect, roaming with pebbles to be used as loom weights, enabling them to work remotely wherever their itinerary would take them.

In Europe, grand tours to Italy and Greece became essential for researching documents and assessing regions to explore. With the taste for the antique ways of life came the science of archaeology with its principles of chronology, typology and stratigraphy, which led to the moulding of the relics in plaster and the careful mending of broken artefacts in glass and clay.

The curiosity cabinet was born for culture's curious elite to display bones and pottery, figurines and fragments of marble and coral. The discovery and excavation of Pompeii furthered the romantic image of archaeology; stimulating the imagination and giving found objects a new aura. Even today, additional scandals about this promiscuous and hedonistic city are being unveiled.

In the 16th century, archaeology became the major science to write history and later it was seen as an important tool to understand national borders and behaviour. Yet it was at the beginning of the 20th century that other theories such as Darwinism permitted prehistoric archaeology to lay its foundations, denoting human evolution with the discovery of Homo Sapiens. Ever since the term prehistory was invented, archaeology changed the way contemporary writers and modern painters conceived the past, present and future, as it liberated wild speculation and imagination in cultural circles.

EXCAVATING FRAGMENTS

At the beginning of our current century, another genre of archaeology has been born; a generation of designers that imagines the remains of unknown periods, narrating the epic adventures of hunters and gatherers, recreating ancient abodes, tools, garments and textiles, and even adopting the Paleo culinary regimen as a healthy diet for the human race. Objects look primitive and are carved and crafted by hand. They have an ancient patina that makes them look authentic. Copies of old façades, furniture constructed like boulders, and the speculation of how our plastics will be found and understood in a far future, each fuel a curiosity for our own cultural history while theoretic studies take flight into an unknown age. Some design is even constructed from very recent excavations, to illustrate the short and devastating history of urban expansion; contemporary remnants that warn about our own possible extinction.

Marc Sadler for Foscarini, Tress, 2009

Jeroen Wand, Phases, 2012-2016

Deltas and riverbanks have inspired children to play with mud since the dawn of time. Clay's warm moisture and slightest resistance to touch make it the most malleable material on the planet. Its generous nature grows life, shapes objects and helps build dwellings in a spontaneous and instinctive manner. In all civilizations, people have learnt how to pommel earthen matter and take the air out of it; pinching little figures, flattening plates, throwing it to form cups and coiling it to create vessels.

Coiling became the way earthenware was produced, using a little water to soften the mud and then firing the pots, changing brown clay into warm terracotta and shades of polished black. To speed up the coiling process, the potter's wheel was invented, giving rhythm and whirl to the technique. Thus, the throwing of ceramics starts with a ball of clay positioned at the centre of the turntable, which the potter rotates with foot power or a mechanical motor. The solid lump of soft matter is centred to open up the mass, then is pressed, squeezed and pulled upwards and outwards into the hollow shape of a container. These abstract organic forms then get features by adding a handle, a lid or some feet and a pair of ears. The artist designs and signs their work by decorating the pieces with incising and carving techniques; the scarification of the clay gives the artefacts character and presence. Painting and glazing obtain a permanent lustre, decorating the containers once they are dried and fired.

At first, primitive urns used to be consolidated in an open bonfire but later the kiln was invented as an oven to raise the hellish temperatures that create dramatic changes in the chemical and mineral aspects of the ceramics. The atmosphere in the kiln is studied to affect the finishes, oxidizing the surfaces by allowing more or less air. As a right of passage, the flames add character and endurance to the products, preparing them for a contained life of household chores, celebrations and rituals.

THROWING EARTH

Clay has become a magic material for autonomous designers, as earthenware and porcelain return to the circles of art and design. A new generation shakes off old shackles and rethinks production processes and designs machines to make this happen. Moving away from the wheel, they invent itineraries for the material to be extruded through pre-designed moulds or pushed through a machine. Clay is even layered by hacked 3D printers into grand volumes, liberating the printing process from its initial material restrictions. Dippings and finishes are scrutinised to find the designer's own handwriting, veiling several expressions all at the same time, within the same design. These objects have a great presence and act like arts & craft items; with intensely coloured furniture and hand-finished vases that are presented to collectors by galleries and fairs.

Kueng Caputa, Sand Chair, 2012

Tom Dixon, Etch Pendant Brass

Metal is an indestructible but malleable material that can be polished to obtain shine and show off its lustrous beauty while conducting warmth and charm. It can be hammered into shape and forged with endurance, opening up a host of possibilities to make sustainable products for the long haul. More than a quarter of the earth's crust is composed from different metals, believed to be the source of its protective magnetic field. Metal has influenced design and architecture to use it in projects from buildings and bridges to tabletop objects and coins. Metals can be recycled indefinitely, minimizing their negative environmental impact, making the choice of its range ultimately sustainable.

As a mineral that is hard by nature, metal becomes fluid when melted at extreme temperatures in order to be poured into shape before it becomes cool and resistant. In many cases, metals don't have all the desired qualities and are combined as alloys to become new materials, melting gold and silver together, titanium and silicon, or nickel and zinc which look like silver once they are brought together as one. These creative intermetallic compounds are solicited for their different traits and might mix the brittle with the sturdy to achieve the ultimate desired character. Often these experiments lend extra value to an otherwise cheaper material, embellishing products with a lustrous coat, such as the Pre-Columbian alloy that mixed copper and gold, giving a golder than gold impression. Pewter, a mixture of tin and copper, became a famous material for plates, bowls and tumblers, and somehow influenced monastic modesty with its matte and unassuming allure. Thus each alloy has impacted its timeframe with its appearance, influencing textiles, textures and even ceramics to follow the lead. Making the materials harder and stronger, resistant to rusting and corrosion, and more attractive in tone and polish, are the main options and solutions humans pursue in these hybrid processes. Today the iron alloys such as stainless steel and cast iron make up the largest quantities and represent the bulk of the mega metal world.

FORGING ALLOY

Aluminium and titanium are for lightweight production and have become the materials of our times. Bronze is the amazing alloy of cupper and arsenic that has given its name to a prehistoric period; since bronze tools, weapons and armour were harder and more durable than stone. Today bronze is making a remarkable revival in the hands of an artistic generation of autonomous designers, keen on the way the matter can be polished to obtain patina and tint. Making simple objects into valuable investments, this current mode for solid shine brings an extra value to design objects. But the handling of these materials is irreverent and explorative, rethinking the need for metal in our contemporary culture. Metal is therefore made lightweight, is recycled from computer waste, is forged into abstraction and soldered into simple shapes. The mood has shifted towards modern modesty and honesty.

Oskar Zieta, Plopp, 2008

Pieke Bergmans, Crystal Virus, 2007

The very first glass product were beads, used as jewellery and money, developed in Mesopotamia, Egypt and Syria, two centuries BC. Making glass is an age-old craft, recognized and invented whenever heated silica sand became liquid and fluid. Humans understood this principle could be guided and perfected, producing vessels, windows and jewellery. Later on the transparent material became artistic and cultural, bestowing the world with the sense of awe that glass can bring on any given day or event. Glass has an innate quality to catch the light and reflect a sense of wonder, creating exciting celebrations. The magic of glass as a vessel can even inspire the very wines, teas or liquors it contains.

Some regions have become so associated with glass that their very name is synonymous with the material. The island of Murano is a household name; having gained prominence in the world glass trade, the Venetian island produces luxurious dinnerware, mirrors and multi-coloured chandeliers. Made from local silica, and processed by soda ash from the Levant, they have a monopoly on the best ingredients to make the finest and clearest qualities of glass. But it is also their capacity to tint the molten matter that makes glass blown in Murano so famous to this day. Another region that has a claim to fame for its crystal production is Bohemia, producing glass that is hand-cut, etched and painted, blown into double-walled sinuous shapes, giving a decorative and baroque aspect to the essential material.

This fragile transparent material is a magical ingredient that creates wonder. Through the ages, glass has taken on other functions and guises, from sturdy beads to romantic roamers, simple light bulbs and high tech skyscrapers. Glass went from being a decorative household item to becoming a building material for the future. The Industrial Age brought mass produced glass products to contain and preserve food as a packaging component; the sober shape of the milk bottle, the sexy shape of the soda bottle as well as the mustard, pickle and jam jars that ooze old-fashioned functionalism, reborn as trendy drink cups today.

BLOWING MAGIC

The principle of heating and taking form has inspired the contemporary development of glass making. The molten material is empowered with human breath, blown into uncontrolled organic shapes, and reinvented by further experiments with the moulding of glass in soil, wooden containers, baskets or found objects. Today a new generation of designers takes the material a step further, treating it with audacity, giving it freedom, liberating it from its confinement. They insist on developing an alternative, more anarchistic aesthetic that brings the material closer to reality and everyday life. Once given this liberty of expression, the heated molten mass starts to coil and coagulate, to oscillate and undulate, to swell, drip and drape, as if it were textile. The magic material is cast in forgotten forms, heated for the reshaping of existing objects and dripped by hand to write another chapter in design history.

Tanja Saeter, Evolving II, 2008

Pauline Esparon, L'Écoucheur, 2019

Fibres are essential for life on earth, since they hold together the tissue structures of plants and animals, which would otherwise fall apart. Most fibrous plant species are native to moist tropical and temperate climates, gifting humanity with their strength, durability, flexibility, ability to adopt colour and resistance to decay. Fibre is a long unruly thread derived and decorticated from palms, plants, grasses and leaves, responsible for yarns such as cotton, linen, jute, raffias and hemp. The more creative materials are often borrowed from wilder plant and palm species such as abaca, pineapple, ramie, cannabis, coconut and sisal, and have served humanity since its inception.

The impetuous fibres of reed, rattan and bamboo have fascinated people because of their headstrong potential to bring shelter, build structures and design objects. They can be split, spun, twined and twisted together into filaments, braided into strings, knotted into rope and woven into wicker. But they can also be matted into sheets to make mats for flooring which continues to be an essential industry in tropical regions. The rebellious and impulsive nature of the plants and palms makes natural fibres lively and present, expressing their own resistant character. They tend to follow the same path to creation, as if guiding the artisan with their own will.

In the beginning, people started to harvest these wild matters to make fences, roofs, dwellings, insulation and ritualistic clothing. Used for protection, the dried materials were layered, coiled, woven and plaited into structures that could beat the weather and survive in dire circumstances. The regions dependant on the harvest of these materials have developed cottage industries; products that are derived and guided by the palms and plants, producing mats, baskets and brooms as well as constructed stools and tables. It is incredible to witness how the same materials are used for similar purposes in several continents of the world; from Portugal to Japan to Africa, roofs and raincoats are almost identical, humans seem to have come to similar conclusions over time and distance.

GATHERING FIBRE

Recently, a revived interest in fibre manufacturing has set the tone for versatile nomadic products that correspond to a contemporary preference for lightweight natural products. Macramé, matting, basketry and open weave furniture in materials such as rattan and bamboo are inspiring designers to travel afar and work with local artisans and women's collectives; drawing upon centuries of indigenous knowledge and craft expertise. The call of this dry-handed and organic aesthetic brings the product closer to nature and its origin, drawing people towards a wilder future. Notably flax is having a great impact on design and is again farmed and spun locally on a small scale; designed with woven, tasselled, fringed and compact systems of making. At times the raw materials are compressed into composite matter that is moulded into robust but flexible shapes. Resilient fibres from palms and other plants are bent into moving structures and open baskets – all new forms of nesting.

Diana Scherer, Hyper Rhizome #2 (detail), 2020

As long as the human eye has scrutinized its environment, the interaction between nature and people has existed. Roaming, gathering and hunting have guided humbling experiences in the natural world, reigning over the power of people. The way birds make nests, otters build dams, cats create dens and spiders weave webs has inspired design to study biomimicry, soliciting these recipes of a higher order. Thus humans made dams and lakes, appropriated caves as living spaces, started to weave textiles and braided fibre into dwellings.

The protection shields of animals invited the design of armour while the tribal cohesion of animals inspired new social rules to keep communities together. The dangers of the outer world inspired fear and defence as essential human traits, building and further developing intuition. Nature was also seen as the generous provider of water and fruits, nuts and roots, even mushrooms and plants as hallucinating agents. Its molluscs became the provider of mother of pearl, its minerals a source of embellishment, its skins and horns took on the function of gris-gris, and its grasses became our first garments. Feathers represented spiritual ascent and direct access to heaven while pebbles translated the grounding belief principles of the origins of life. Water and the moon reflected each other and called for narcissism to bloom.

Gradually humans mastered their environment and wanted to tame it. In the earliest agricultural settlements, mankind invented tools and mechanical devices powered by the exploitation of nature; wind, animals and people. Since that time, the human brain has never stopped innovating and overhauling the social and natural order. With the Industrial Revolution, this movement proliferated, and with the mass creation of goods came the mass creation of wealth and waste. Now in the digital age, these processes haven't ceased, introducing never-ending overconsumption and overproduction, and uncontainable pollution levels that jeopardize the survival of our species. It's clearly time to abolish these infernal systems and come to our senses, to stop travelling and hoarding, instead creating time and leisure for humans to thrive. The time for unnovation has arrived.

GROWING DESIGN

Since the turn of the century, several designers decided to ask nature to help them give shape, such as in vases built by bees in their own hives, wallpaper perforated by gnawing mice and moths employed to decompose fibres for new recycling methods. The products from plants and animals are discovered to create new matter; cellulose and collagen amongst the two most promising components in material research. Sea salt is used to grow crystals on objects and limestone is solicited to create new rock. The earth is turned inside out to find new natural sources, from harvesting seaweed to create vegan materials to exploiting mushrooms for their mycelium. Nature is requested to develop roots to grow products and harvest design. The promise of future design farming seems to become a reality, where bio-engineered production will no longer damage the earth. At last, nature and man can again live together in harmony.

Violaine Buet, installation (detail), Salone del Mobile, 2019

Dick van Hoff, VEEG, 2014

A LABOUR OF LOVE AN ACT OF FAITH A PROOF OF WILL A TOKEN OF LIFE

At the entrance to the manufacturing plant stand the metal cabinets in different colours; installed in a line, patiently awaiting their function as guardians of personal belongings or corporate secrets. At first view, the lockers are sampled from a catalogue of industrial goods, ready to store worker's clothing, office papers or technical components. They have the volume, finish and presence of a uniquely industrial cabinet, serially produced by Lensvelt and available in a series of matte paints that can be used together as a family or as a unique highlight in a functional interior. But something else sets these lockers apart and makes them treasures of contemporary design.

Upon closer inspection, these practical containers turn into cabinets of curiosity through the added interest of a giant bronze key; inviting all kinds of people to use the otherwise working class objects.

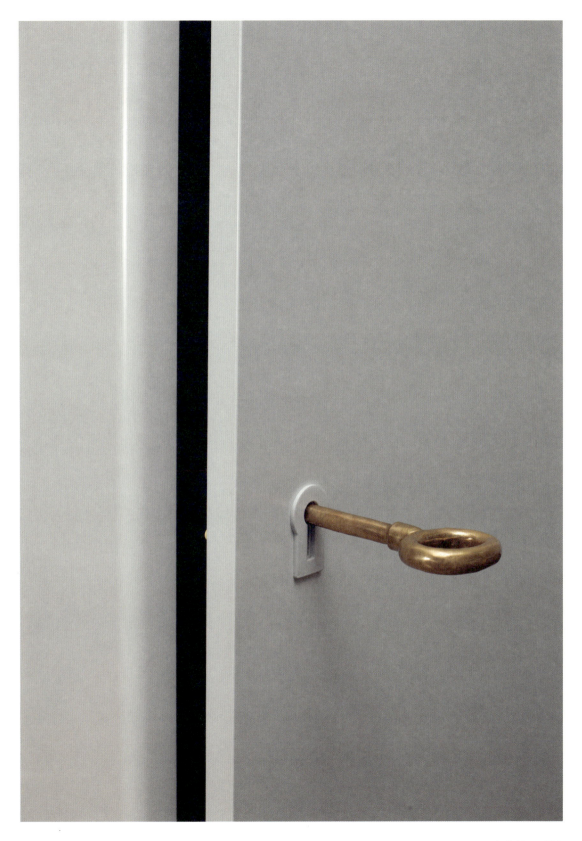

Job Cabinet, 2011

The key is part of Studio Job's idiom that has always aimed to elevate the ordinary and reconsider the functional, turning farmers' pitchforks, soldiers' swords and chefs' casseroles into polished bronze collectibles. Purchasing this locker therefore has a double meaning, combining function and frivolity; where the value of the golden Job key largely pays back the item's initial price.

A surreal sense of humour is displayed in this iconic design piece, representing the best of Studio Job, where the standard is shocked out of its lethargy and infused with new tongue-in-cheek energy. The combination of largesse with an ordinary item creates tension, making these lockers witnesses of our times when high and low unite to rethink the nobility in labour.

CABINETS OF CURIOSITY
Studio Job

Job Cabinet, 2011

The broom is a centuries-old tool for cleaning dust on floors. It has become an instrument of reform and represents a clear and cleaner vision. Overhauling the design discipline from scratch, this broom stands as a symbol for cleaning up our act. Its sweeping qualities translate as a resolution for major change. The large brushes scrub up old adagios in favour of new practices. The tall handle permits a hands-on approach to set new rules for work to become a labour of love, including taking care of people and the planet too.

Transporting witches and dreams, the broomstick has magical powers to shift perceptions and initiate alternative realities. It heralds a total overhaul of production, with great reverence for human and material resources. Used as a partner to dance with, it also illustrates social inclusion and a playful way to learn how to exchange with others.

Designed by the radical and matter-of-fact Dick van Hoff, this oversized broom for sweeping up waste and dusting off design is made by social workshops in the Netherlands, and is an important part of the Social Label collection. Constructed from obsolete parts from a bike factory, the broom is literally tidying up its own waste, which in itself makes it a powerful thing to speak of; wiping the past clean for a sustainable fresh start.

SWEEPING CHANGE
Dick van Hoff

VEEG, 2014

About a Worker

She is of Chinese descent and he is French; the countries of continued communist rule and ferocious workers' unions, which combine the notions of employment as a common duty and work laws as a protected right. During their education, they joined forces and set out to transform the core values of labour. The idea was simple but the execution challenging, encountering disbelief and negation from their audience and partners; therefore they must be lauded for their motivating energy and perseverance. Through their inspiring creations and workshops in the art and design disciplines, they managed to express their perspective as a new form of social activism. Thus branding their destiny – About a Worker – along the way.

The question that Kim Hou and Paul Boulenger asked themselves was why workers were not involved in the stages of research and design, and why their experienced voices were never heard? They estimated that the loss of knowledge and creative energy was a negative for any company or brand, but also a negative for the experiences of the workforce; their intuitive instincts excluded from the manufacturing process, resulting in disinterest, going trough the motions as usual, without a passion for participation.

Saint-Denis Collection, 2017

Their first attempt – and Hou's graduation project – brought them to France to visit a renowned producer of worker's garments in Saint Denis. Impeccable true blue workwear is famous around the world and recently cool people started to adopt these proven pieces as a new way of dressing, away from mainstream fashion. The duo spoke to management and was reluctantly given permission to do a test run based on their theory.

Hou and Boulenger selected a group of labourers and set them apart for a few weeks of workshops and training, delivering the tools of creativity to the innocent workers that had never really thought about the design of the clothing they made day in, day out. They explained the intricacies of creative practice to them, and conducted field trips to photograph the interesting grids found in architecture and public space as inspiration. With these abstract images in mind, professional mood boards were created, empowering the workers in their first steps up the creative ladder. The dedicated staff started to sketch and imagine, doing samples of stitching and pleating, gathering the sturdy cloth into more sensuous curves. From this research, final garments underwent the new treatments and detailing, upgrading the everyday character of the cloth and clothes. The results far exceeded Hou and Boulenger's expectations, as the energy it unleashed in the participants was palpable in

Shenzhen Collection, 2020

the designs. Jackets were honoured with a pleated peplum or a large frill meandering over one sleeve to lift these garments up and gave them creative status. This happened just before Dior showed identical designs in the same blue, confirming the intuition of the workers on the runway…

Many projects have followed and many will still come, further outlining how it's possible to creatively empower the working class. The two have since taught and collaborated with inmates in a Venetian prison; they created a formidable workwear collection with six members of the logistics team at La Redoute; and also inspired workers in Shenzen's factories to discover their hidden design talents. Even a company producing the famous Charentaise slippers gave in to a makeover. For La Manufacture during Lille 2020, the couple created a pop-up atelier sewing blue work aprons for the exhibition guides and volunteers. Hou and Boulenger crisscross the world to teach students, give lectures and stage installations, all with the goal to inspire others to do the same and bring workers and designers together in the process. Their philosophy just might change the future of labour to become a labour of love.

ABOUT WORKER'S BLUE
About A Worker

Saint-Denis Collection, 2017

It is estimated that there are currently over 30 million refugees and 150 million homeless people around the world. Bas Timmer has heroically stepped up to take on this daunting matter through his humanitarian work. He acknowledges that he cannot fix the issue alone, but offers "a short-term solution to a long-term problem", believing that everyone has the right to warmth and protection. The trained fashion designer turned his skills to starting Sheltersuit; an initiative that provides compassion and shelter to the needy so that they can escape freezing to death on the streets. The suit combines the practicality of a hooded jacket, pockets and sleeves with a comfortable sleeping bag, all folding up into a backpack. Timmer was motivated to make the first prototype following the death of a friend's father in his hometown of Enschede. Shocked by the realisation that homelessness existed so close by, and driven by an altruistic desire to help more people, the Dutch boy wonder founded an organisation that has since given away tens of thousands of Sheltersuits in the Netherlands, Lesbos, Sarajevo, South Africa and the United States.

Sheltersuits are sewn together by volunteers and the unemployed, mainly refugees that have fled conflict zones with their tailoring skills intact. The colourblocked suits are constructed from wind- and waterproof fabrics donated by tent factories and recycled from fashion sources; even scavenged when necessary from large outdoor

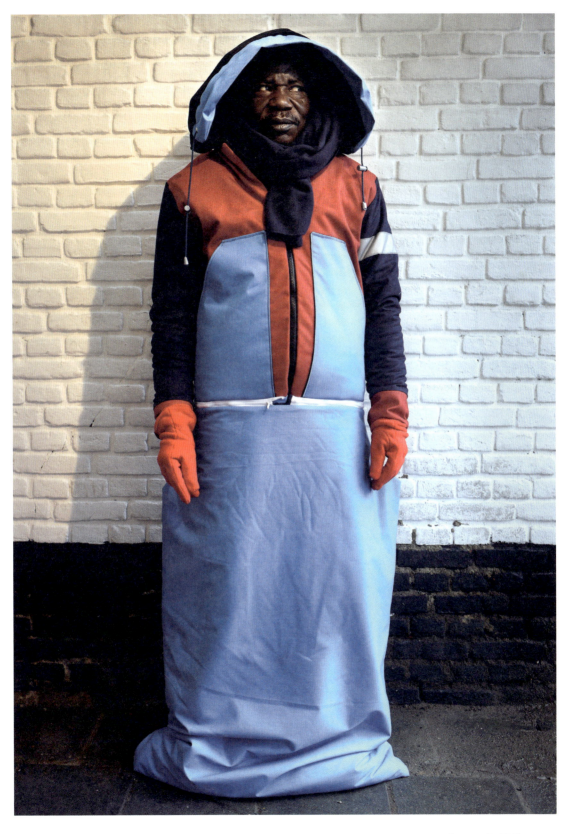

Sheltersuit, 2014–present

Sheltersuit, 2014–present

Sheltersuit, 2014–present

festivals where camping gear is often abandoned. Thus the project also absorbs textile waste and gives fairly paid work to communities that are starting over.

Timmer's attention to detail illustrates his innate empathy for the others, ensuring there are children's sizes and that his designs include pockets for cell phones. He recently established ateliers in Cape Town, where a lighter weight version of the Sheltersuit was developed in collaboration with Design Indaba. These new prototypes push the Sheltersuit forward, improving it for the better each time.

Members of the public can crowdfund or purchase a Sheltersuit online; doing good with their intentions and becoming part of the answer. October 10th marks World Homeless Day and in 2020, Timmer's team is spearheading an international sleep-out to raise further awareness around this mounting social crisis. As unemployment and homelessness regretfully rise in many places, Sheltersuit offers a glimmer of hope. Timmer's dream is that microfactories like his will flourish around the globe, so that humanity can help the most vulnerable in society. By campaigning and expanding his inspiring programme, he is doing just that.

PROVIDING HOPE
Bas Timmer

The Human Trace, 2016–2017

As with any technological chapter in history, the digital age has brought both positives and negatives to society; while communication seems more fluid, many people feel increasingly alienated and alone. The arrival of artificial intelligence is perhaps the largest threat to communities – many jobs are set to disappear, replacing experience and intuition with algorithms and systemisation. To confront these issues, anthropologist Ewa Klekot and ceramicist Arkadiusz Szwed collaborated on a project that celebrates the hand of the worker on a production line; emphasising human presence and ingenuity rather than trying to erase it.

In *The Human Trace*, one of Poland's oldest porcelain factories was disrupted for a weeklong experiment. Could one illustrate the number of times tableware is touched by its makers during manufacturing? After asking the staff at Ćmielów to wear gloves dipped in a cobalt salt solution, fingerprints and fine smudges left their mark across the production pieces; albeit invisibly until reaching the kiln when they turned a deep

The Human Trace, 2016-2017

blue. The resulting motifs look random and echo the most abstract of patterns. They magically materialise in contrast to the grand traditional shapes of the collection: elegant teacups and saucers, scalloped plates and platters, generous tureens and tall spouted teapots. The fluid hand movements and fast gestures in the making process are thus forever recorded, reminding all to see just how important craftsmanship is to industrial production – and why we must protect it.

Klekot and Szwed documented the study through writings, black and white portraits of the workers and a short film. These elements form part of a broader mission called *People from the Porcelain Factory* that has toured design weeks around the world. Like the blue imprints, this research pays homage to human touch and the crafting of objects with soul.

HUMAN TRACE
People from
the Porcelain Factory

The Human Trace, 2016-2017

Kom, 2015

As a mother, designer, educator and social agitator Petra Janssen – working in concert with her husband Edwin Vollebergh – has a great and happy life, punctuated by creative challenges and collaborations with friends, her local region and the city of Den Bosch. Their house is in a restored manufacturing plant with a central kitchen where work and life go hand in hand, as does teaching, designing and production. Their colourful interior is filled with flowers, good food and design icons. Their life together as Studio Boot is filled to the brim.

Although always optimistic, this diligent woman was no longer content with the perfection of her life and tried to come to terms with her dissatisfaction. Soul searching through the unease she felt around current hedonistic societal trends, she considered other methods to design, produce and be of service to the world. She therefore initiated a festival for new ways of building and living, and the experiment laid bare the urgent need for alternative social values. Invited architects, artists and designers set out to build a village on dilapidated terrain, and without knowing it they actually designed the future of the region.

Woodworks, a social workshop from the area, was also included to craft their dwelling and wanted to mimic Piet Hein Eek's iconic furniture. *We can do that too*, was their thought. Janssen suggested they ask permission and generous Hein Eek agreed and gave them technical drawings to fully understand the design structure. After the festival concluded, all participants joined forces and the first Social Label product called *HOUT* was launched. Janssen and Simone Kramer became the initiators and guardians of this original concept to design labour. In their quest for better products and higher goals, they discovered the multiple social workshops in the Netherlands, often

Kom, 2015

producing uninteresting products and omitting the creative forces of their craftspeople. With different degrees of disabilities and health issues come different ideas for products that can best fit the people at work, bringing them the joy of making a meaningful product range together with selected designers and workshop supervisors. When people create something beautiful and can demonstrate their achievements, it boosts their sense of self-esteem and encourages them to use their skills to participate in society.

Once the inventory of possibilities was mapped out, they started to ask more designer friends to participate in the process. Their adhesion was overwhelming, the enthusiasm palpable, and their collective minds were set on changing the world of work. Design became a vehicle for experimentation and analysis in terms of material, function and knowledge. Through the integration of different rhythms, skills and other ways of making, the initiative's products gained a new value for the maker and the designer alike. Social Label's "design by doing" now involves fifteen workshops with 150 craftspeople and 17 designers.

The first and amazingly beautiful object that saw the light of day was a broom designed by Dick van Hoff, manufactured from obsolete bike parts, repurposing the brightly tinted metal frames. The broom is extra wide, ultra long and very dense, and becomes an object that doesn't want to go back into the cupboard, elevating sweeping into a daily delight.

The next step was evident since a place to sell both the products and the concept became essential for further growth. In the city of Tilburg they found an empty vestige from the region's industrial past and received permission to create a cultural shopping destination there, in collaboration with other brands and creative studios. Here, the full measure of Janssen's moral compass and creative entrepreneurial

Kom, 2015

skills joint forces, bringing a broader audience to this bold brand of social justice and inclusion. Many designers and workshops have followed, within an open design lab where they invent new solutions for collaborating and living together; a space where workers, customers and designers challenge and learn from one another.

Possibly, Social Label's most popular and commercial project is the production of tabletop pieces for tea and coffee, with cups, saucers, milk jugs and pots. A group of dedicated young people living with down syndrome create their own pieces of craft using stickers designed by Vollebergh that are assembled in personal ways by the different workers. They freely mix a sailor's tattoo with a romantic heart, let birds fly out of cages, surround a handgun with peace flowers, give wings to a wheelchair, and add daring words and endearing mottos. The result is a contemporary interpretation of Delft blue, challenging tradition…

At times during work sessions, the available images are scrutinized and innovated by requests from the craftspeople for more audacious pictures of curvaceous sexy women or a punk skull. With lots of laughter and love, the pieces are decorated to add pleasure to designated tables, turning entertaining into a pastime of discovery. The biggest fan of the project is Queen Máxima who opened the space and sat at the worktable to witness the creative process, overwhelmed by the simple yet sublime way of teaching creativity to all of humankind. Social Label will bring hope further into the world since a travelling exhibition is currently in the works.

DESIGNING LABOUR
Social Label

Designing for all of society means leaving no one behind. From education to healthcare, hospitality and manufacturing, social design encourages employment opportunities that welcome and empower the disabled, disadvantaged or marginalised. Empathy is perhaps design's greatest force, and Roland Pieter Smit channels this quality by putting the needs of others first. In *Wolwaeren*, he designed a collection of seven pure wool blankets that can be comfortably made by artisans with mental or physical impairments, fabricating beautiful products while honouring inclusion.

Smit conceived a weaving loom that is easy to operate. He analysed the textile production chain and learned how different yarn gauges are suitable depending on the person's dextrousness: thicker ones are manageable for those with down syndrome while autistic workers can manage thinner yarns too. The project has grown into a long term initiative, selling blankets and cushions around the world while providing a steady source of income to all those involved. This extends to the sheep farmers of Texel, a small island north of Amsterdam, whose struggling wool industry has been supported by *Wolwaeren*'s orders that offer a fair market price for the fleece. Recently, Smit started *Made by Scorlewald*, a series of textile, metal and wood objects crafted in workshops for those with special needs, and worked with local clay potters in the Kathmandu Valley. Dedicated to the elevation of handskills and collaboration, Smit helps improve people's lives while sustaining true connections between each of these craft communities.

CRAFTING WITH COMMUNITY
Roland Pieter Smit

Wolwaeren, 2010-present

Wolwaeren, 2010–present

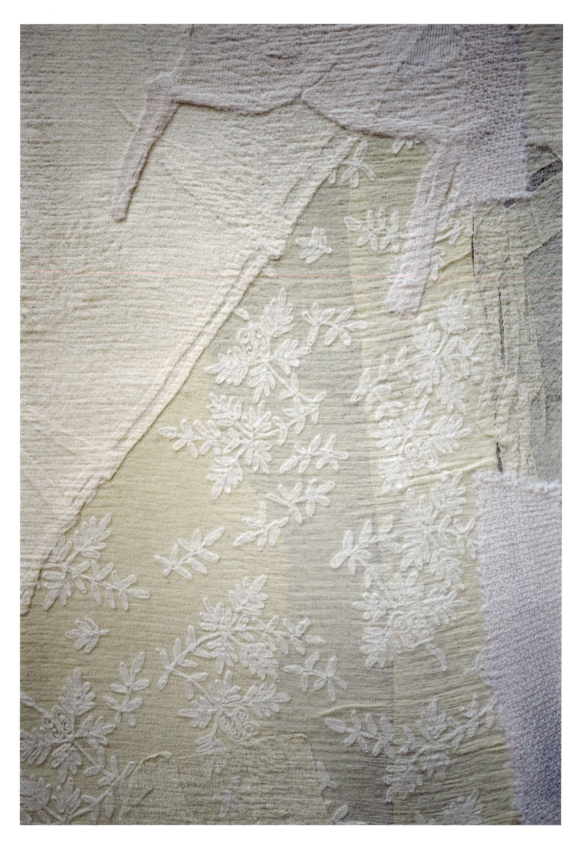

Ecru Two, 2019

"Textiles and apparel have a huge environmental impact and our industry's current model is unsustainable. We're using up natural resources faster than they can be renewed. We're making more and more stuff. And after each season, we toss out the old and move onto what's next. Where does this mountain of used and unsold clothes go?" These are some of the concerns by American fashion designer Eileen Fisher; she wants to create an industry that actually helps restore the planet and it all starts with her company taking responsibility for what it makes – and where it ends up. Fisher believes the future is circular.

WASTE NO MORE is part of the solution, representing the philosophy of conscious consumption. The zero-waste initiative brings together creativity and innovation, architects and designers, ethics and business. Under the wing of artist and creative director Sigi Ahl, the project transforms damaged clothes from the Eileen Fisher brand, elevating them into artworks, wall coverings, acoustic panels, upholstery, pillows, garments, bags and other accessories.

This ambitious programme has bought back well over one million garments. They are carefully sorted by colour and fibre in the company's micro manufacturing plant: the Tiny Factory, located in a beautiful Stanford White building on the banks of the Hudson River in Irvington, New York. Waste No More combines an appreciation of valuable renewable materials with an artisanal approach to craft and technology, including the development of unique needle-punch felting techniques that do not require water, producing a range of textures and weights for various uses, always coloured in the original shades of the waste.

Recent works focus on the symbolic power and emotional depth of white, from the clarity of bright white to the warmth of ecru – and even unexpected faint greys and dirty whites. The creative team scoured thousands of garments to select the perfect linen, cotton, wool and silks used. Each piece is the result of a meticulous process in which hand-sheared scraps and discarded materials have been layered to create unique compositions.

The use of whites alone has laid bare the handwriting of the different ways of shredding the cloth by hand or by scissors or both; thus defining the visual language, similar to the paint strokes of a brush. Learning from trial and error, experimentation and chance, Ahl has grown an impressive body of artwork that is now bought by collectors, museums, developers and hotels.

White symbolizes simplicity. As a spiritual hue, it represents renewal, cleansing, focus and serenity – and offers a much-needed antidote to chaotic socio-political times. White also stands for illumination and reincarnation, both central to the regenerative concept of Waste No More. The works evoke a sanctuary, exploring the meaning of aesthetic activism while confronting the unsustainable model of the fashion industry. Where others see waste, they see possibility.

CIRCULAR BY DESIGN
Waste No More

Ecru One, 2018

Selvedge is well known as the edge of fabric that is cut off during the industrial weaving process; a significant fringe of the global textile industry that amounts to 10% of carbon emissions and 5% of the world's waste. Salem van der Swaagh collects discarded selvedge strips from various European carpet factories and wool mills, and weaves them by hand into highly-tactile rugs and pillows. The design process begins after receiving the yarns from the industry, which are never the same. This textural diversity runs through the tufts in each unique creation; a process akin to weaving a painting that communicates origin and time.

Van der Swaagh is a talented colourist and has worked in several esteemed design studios since graduating from her design studies, yet the hand-knot rugs in her personal practice are shaded in the neutral colours of undyed wool. She believes hand weaving is a potent vehicle for connecting to the immediate environment that surrounds us. It is at once practical and poetic, ancient and sustainable. The ever-present human spirit that seeks expression manifests itself in the art of hand weaving.

SAVAGE SELVEDGE
Salem van der Swaagh

Rug_01_Golden Fade, 2018

Rug_05_Twine, 2018

Today, we live in an overabundance of goods in our consumer society. This is especially true in the fashion industry. Fast fashion brands churn out clothes made with cheap materials and encourage quick responses to their products in order to maintain rapid rates of growth, providing immediate satisfaction at a low cost. However, with only 1% of these clothes being recycled, the poor quality and low sustainability of fast fashion has lead to massive ethical and environmental issues.

Aleelang was a brand by the Korean fashion designer Sun Lee. When her clothes were sold at the Hyundai department store in Seoul, she suddenly realized the insurmountable number of clothes that were being displayed, hers included. Behind the beautiful display windows, clothes are nothing but layers of fabric that overflow and get thrown out once the season passes. Ever since, her design practice has explored contemporary topics through the lens of the fashion industry and questioned the relationships between humans and fashion, tradition and nature.

Consumption of Heritage addresses the status quo, challenging the values of consumers and producers alike. *What are we wearing? What clothes do we make? How and why are we making them?* Lee tackles these notions through her own heritage. Since the 1960s, the industrialization and globalisation of the Korean fashion industry drove traditional textiles and craft out of its regional place. Due to the diminishing number of local artisans, a few master craftsmen became highly regarded artists and craft became seen as a fine art, instead of being a part of everyday life. Lee is interested in bringing back the culture of craft to society and making it relevant for our lives.

The garments in the collection are made mainly from traditional Hansan mosi fabric and hanji paper. They are designed for specific situations and purposes based on the relationship between the wearer and clothing, consumption and disposability. Derived from plants, both mosi and hanji represent the ephemeral philosophy of life and death. Like a tree with roots deeply anchored in the soil that brings delicate leaves and beautiful flowers, mosi and hanji also embody consciousness and harmony. This natural balance is realized in the clothing through a layering process, in which the combinations of and interactions between the two materials create a higher level of appreciation for quality, adaptability and context.

EVERYDAY CRAFT
Sun Lee

Consumption of Heritage, 2019

Scraps from sentimental encounters and an intimate connection to other people's garments are at the core of Femke van Gemert's anthropological textile practice. She has intuitively invented her medium from scratch and recycles materials by ripping bits and pieces of fabrics; dissecting and reconstructing her findings through weaving. The dense visual language that results from her art resonates with her affinity for the human condition.

Her critique on waste is akin to the beauty born from leftovers and decay, often evoking a melancholic mood. In her studio, she weaves wall panels, tapestries, installations and site-specific soft wall coverings. Van Gemert notes that every piece of textile she uses has been eaten, digested and discarded by society, and for some private commissions, the remnants can even come from the client's belongings.

From one donation, van Gemert received white lace leftovers from the Amsterdam Museum. While washing, drying and selecting the pieces, the artist dreamed of 17th century portraits as well as the black lace worn by seductive femmes in contemporary music and culture. These contrasting notions translated into *Dreaming*, a three-dimensional cubic installation dipped in black dye. Black is of course the most common colour van Gemert receives, due to the tone's commercial success. She sees black as the ultimate spatial colour, "everything and nothing at the same time". This is evident in *Beau Monde in Black* where tennis nets are woven over with unwanted black garments; an abstract void steeped deep in connotations and textures.

TEXTILE DREAMING
Femke van Gemert

Dreaming, 2013

What's in a name? Harris is very traditional English tweed yet Daniel Harris is a semi-traditional young Englishman that has an incredible passion for textile looms, and as a consequence, for cloth. Therefore it was only logic that Harris would weave Harris tweeds one day.

While others collect vintage cars, he collects discarded textile making machinery, accumulating several looms to restore them as one perfectly working specimen. Travelling all over Britain, he is often gifted with heavy and rusted colossal machines, or they are sold to him for a little amount; to be freed from the burden of storage. The countryside is riddled with remnants from the Industrial Age that are ready to be reinvented, and he invites future collectors and entreprenaeurs to do the same.

When his hobby outgrew his initial workshop, he decided to take the plunge and start up a mill in London, the first textile plant to return to the city in over a hundred years. There, he restores his looms, feeds his cat and does textile making. He learns how to select yarns, how to construct and how to finish, delving deep into the geometric secrets of warp and weft. He hacks antiquated looms to produce almost forgotten qualities in cloth; structures and compositions from a faraway past, dusted off and renewed, adopted for our time.

His ethos seems to counter the short-sighted reality of a price-driven society that outsources its textiles. Yet his belief in quality and service has made him successful amidst the worst aesthetic, financial and environmental crisis ever in fashion. His sturdy qualities defy the throw-away mentality of most, since his knowledge

Daniel Harris at the London Cloth Company mill

The London Cloth Company, 2011–present

honours the exceptional history of the woven world. He is a gift to our century; teaching us that small is good and that gain can exist without greed. That work can be a joy and how doing business can become a pleasure. That labour and love belong to one another and should be cherished. His enthusiasm is engaging and his boyish charm helps encourage others to do the same. The next step will be to produce clothes from his own fabrics, to have a fully integrated micro brand. His drive is unstoppable and he is now tackling the first semi-automatic looms and one day he might even rekindle the very first textile computers…

Donations and the accumulation of more machines keep forcing him into larger premises, but still within the city limits of London. Thus the name London Cloth Company can be preserved and perhaps become a household term; an example amongst other young brands that want to embrace a certain formality in traditional clothes, counterbalancing streetwear's endless hoodies. When collaborating with Tiger of Sweden, he studies the punk symbolism in clans woven on the diagonal; and for Comme des Garçons, he investigates the funk in sturdier tweeds, as worn during the War years. These made-to-measure weavings now also reach other brands such as Ralph Lauren and Hardy Amies; houses that share a passion for the past. A passion that leads to quality of cloth, manufactured on a more local and creative level.

INNER CITY CLOTH
Daniel Harris

The London Cloth Company, 2011–present

Daniel Harris at the London Cloth Company mill

As a textile designer and an illustrator, Liuxu Luo uses laser cutting and a sewing machine to make lacelike, three-dimensional patterns, unfolding from two-dimensional embroidery. She creates romantic installations that express beauty like she believes plants and sunlight do, thereby changing the atmosphere to be tranquil and vivid. *Poetry Plant* is a vibrant example of Luo's unique voice; it is a piece in which patchwork and embroidery are applied to transparent layers of cloth. The effect plants have on people is a subject she explored in collaboration with a poet who gave prose to her piece. The poem, *I Like a Tall Tree*, is read aloud as a performance next to her ethereal pieces to give them context.

Recently graduating with a Textiles MFA at Parsons in New York, Luo is passionate about incorporating mediums such as painting, watercolour and craft into her creative practice. She sees herself as a collector; fascinated by beautiful small things like handmade materials, tiny antiques and what others might call garbage or *wuyong*, the Mandarin word for useless. Luo also developed a set of onionskin-dyed garments where the silhouettes are inspired by traditional Chinese layered costumes, echoing the way an onion is built layer by layer. In her project, *Wandering Home*, she used textiles as a physical form of narration, literally creating a wandering home. Natural dyed cotton, silk, ribbon and yarn are interwoven and knit into a mixed media installation that includes laser-cut flowers and a bamboo structure.

NEW IMPRESSIONISM
Liuxu Luo

Wandering Home, 2019-2020

Wandering Home, 2019-2020

Wandering Home, 2019-2020

Vlisco Recycled Carpet samples, 2015

For over 170 years, Vlisco has been the world's most renowned mill specialising in mechanised wax prints. In 1844, the company acquired its first block-printing machine, and was able to mimic labour-intensive hand-drawn Javanese batiks with such precision that they were even preferred in the Dutch East Indies. Following a global recession in the 1870s and a decline in trade with that market, Vlisco's textiles were sold in other places that had an intrinsic appreciation for prints such as Japan and Sweden. In the 1880s, the company started selling in Africa, especially in Central and West Africa where Vlisco's bright and graphic language has since become synonymous with made-to-measure African style.

To maintain its position as the global leader in industrial wax printing, quality control is paramount at Vlisco and the slightest misprint during the 27 manufacturing steps is reason to discard the cloth. This regretful wasteful process concerned the designer Simone Post, whose regular work delves deep into colour and two-dimensionality, having collaborated with companies such as Adidas and Kvadrat. Since Post strives to preserve crafts while promoting sustainability, it was only natural that her extensive research for Vlisco lead to a sustainable solution; a perfect antidote to the costly and time-consuming process of destroying the defective yardage. Inspired by the side view of Vlisco's oversized round production rolls, her rug designs are circular in every sense. Challenged to never reveal the printing flaws, the fabrics are cut into strips, folded and coiled; creating floor rugs in myriad compositions that are each unique, beautifying the leftover fabric by transforming it into a new item for the home or public space.

FROM FLAW TO FLOOR
Simone Post

Although he produces objects, Anton Alvarez is not a product designer. He has turned the design profession around to become an inventor of machines instead. He wants to be liberated from industrial and traditional constraints, and therefore started his own mechanical workshop. Alvarez's pieces focus on the design of systems and the creation of tools and processes. When he studied design at Konstfack in Stockholm and completed his masters at the Royal Academy in London, the curious young man was immersed in the worlds of textile as well as product design, planting the seeds for his first adventure into manufacturing, making his initial *Thread Wrapping Machine* to spin thousands of metres of cotton yarn around the frames of wood, metal or plastic.

Here, cotton threads and glue replace joints and screws to hold the objects together; as if it were a cast for a broken bone. The exciting rhythm of the turning is reminiscent of a potter's wheel where the human body and the mechanical movement become one, giving shape to the material. In creative symbiosis, Alvarez decides on colour and structure while the wrapping machine decides on density and pattern. From one piece of wood, Alvarez then

Thread Wrapping Machine (detail), 2012

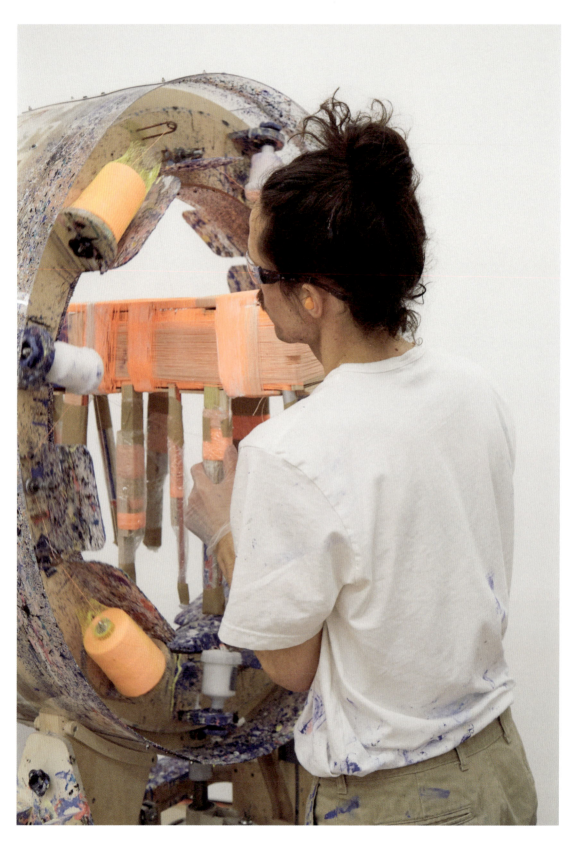

Thread Wrapping Machine, 2012

deviates and adds other pieces that are tightly connected by the coiling process; giving his creative dance its own wild energy, embedded in these abstract sculptural pieces. From endearing stools to stretched out benches and towering totems, his work eventually resembles a forest of multi-coloured beings in dialogue, complimenting and completing one another.

Always his own curious self, the Chilean-Swede seems to be able to blend his two origins into one aesthetic, bringing the instinctive language of the Americas to the structured modernism of Scandinavia. A new step has brought him to ceramic making, and again he refuses to follow tradition, scheming up a device that can take away the burden of labour. Inspired by ice cream machines, he has created a powerful tool that can extrude clay through bold regular grids, to become colourful columns and vessels frozen in different stages of draping and folding – as if experiencing visual vertigo. Like tokens of a lost civilization, the wrapped furniture balances the soft sculptures, fuelling a futurist dynamic.

VISUAL VERTIGO
Anton Alvarez

TTWMS, 2016

Skin Collection, 2011

Recycling is at the heart of many of Pepe Heykoop's designs; turning waste into wonder and making sense out of disparate ingredients. Shocked by the amount of discarded material generated when manufacturing leather products such as sofas, accessories and garments – some 25% is lost in offcuts – he started to forge new upholstery on unwanted objects. Since 2011, the *Skin* collection has covered up office furniture, vanities, benches, rocking chairs and lamps; a new skin that gives a second life to the things we shed as a society. Sometimes, the sewn together hide membranes even merge two items together; creating strange hybrids that turn trash into treasure.

During the 2020 lockdown, he collected thrown-away appliances and furniture parts – including chairs, printers and a spinning wheel – to invent a drawing-machine he christened the *Handwriter*. In an age when designers are considering whether technology directs possibilities – or the other way around – his conceptual approach to circular design previews a time when machines will become an extension of the body, expressing craft techniques while the hand still remains in control, connected to the imagination.

RAGS TO RITCHES
Pepe Heykoop

Skin Collection, 2011

Skin Collection, 2011

Contemporary culture has reached a turning point; finally demanding real change on ecological issues and opening up greener perspectives in all facets of society. In design, sustainable materials now seek circular systems, often conceived with multiple uses in brain. To combat the waste of single-use products, valuable resources are being transformed and reincarnated by a new generation of conscious thinkers.

Dirk Vander Kooij is an award-winning designer, most renowned for the extrusion of reclaimed synthetics, producing chairs, tables, lighting fixtures and accessories. Working as both a craftsman and inventor, he marries machine and the hand while fostering an honest expression of regenerated materials. The recycling process suddenly becomes animated and enchanting, with the agile aide of a de-commissioned robot that the designer has hacked to coil his zero waste furniture and objects, recomposed from almost everything such as plastic bottles, chocolate moulds, headlights, skylight parts and the insides of refrigerators. As such, vander Kooij's made-to-order micro factory is making a macro impact.

ME & MY ROBOT
Dirk Vander Kooij

Changing Vase, 2013

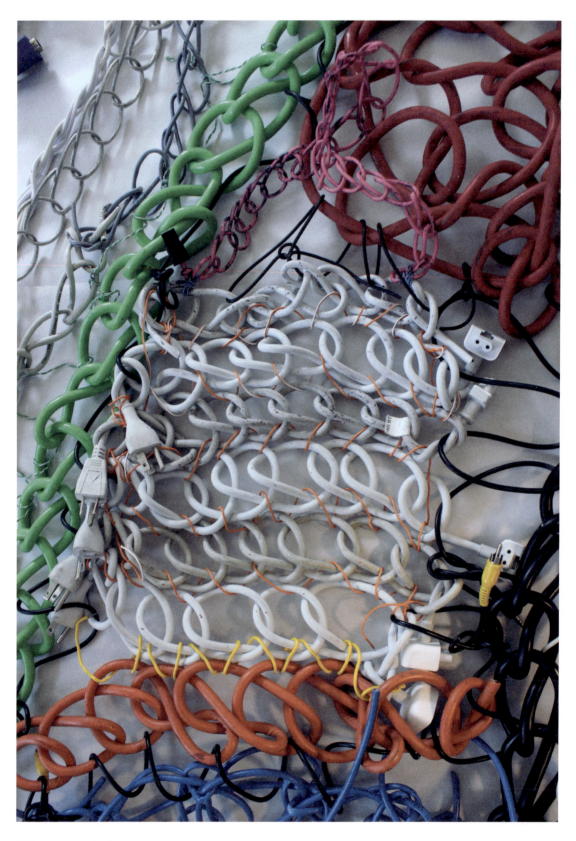

With long ash-coloured hair and the palest of skin, he looks like a pop star and is very slim, very fluid and very stylish, with an understated grunge aesthetic that also defines his work. He looks at the underbelly of society as his field of research and sees beauty in the decadent decay of overconsumption and overproduction. Peter Salera gets his inspiration in the steaming dirty streets of New York. He samples debris like anyone else plucks flowers or collects pebbles; for him, our waste is his wealth of inspirational materials. Paper, plastic, nylon and rubber define his streetwise language, taken from discarded packaging, found furniture and miles of computer chords that he skilfully gathers in huge knitted rugs that work as a vortex able to absorb the guilt for our excessive behaviour. People are moved by this awesome testimony to trash.

   The beauty and strength he derives from the e-waste wires is astounding as he mixes colours such as dirty white and neon bright, as he blends aspects as transparent

Amalgamated Earth Progeny No. 49351, 2019

and rubberized, and as he uses the adaptors as amulets to animate the surface with rummaged fragments and frayed fringes. Knitted on oversized needles and with able hands, this labour of love took several months of accumulating ever more waste; choosing interesting details and connecting the materials with various stitches of knitting.

The two master/slave data-encoding outlets are at the centre of his work, as a critique on the common tech reference to situations where one entity controls another, anticipating the continued importance of inclusivity where the use of hateful words is scrutinized and replaced by the building of a more holistic society. Salera's work certainly projects another world of trash and treasures where values are turned around and where the underdog becomes the creative hero. Taking care of the planet at the same time.

SALERA'S SLANG
Peter Salera

Amalgamated Earth Progeny No. 49351, 2019

The accumulated shapes and disparate surfaces in Kostas Lambridis' spectacular *Elemental Cabinet* are quite monumental. It is his contemporary interpretation of the 18th century baroque *Badminton Cabinet*; which at $36 million is regarded as the most expensive piece of furniture ever sold. "It communicates the wealth, elitism and aristocracy of its time," says Lambridis of the original. Realised to scale in the same dimensions as the antique, Lambridis' collaged incarnation communicates a different idea; highly decorative yet also critical of the world we live in. From concrete and stone to ceramics, wood and plastic, the tower is made of juxtaposed ingredients and includes a clock reconstructed from textiles and e-waste. This non-hierarchical approach to materials generates an aesthetic order out of our disentangled, chaotic social landscape. What will this piece tell future generations who look back to 2017 when it was made?

Following a visit to see the first cabinet in Vienna, Lambridis made a 3D scan of it before composing his eclectic version. Much like an artisanal atelier, his Athens studio is now equipped to craft woodwork, metalwork, stonework and glass. In the accompanying *Elemental* chaise and chandelier, brass, steel, stained glass, neon tubes, plastics and leather all combine to continue this expressive collection of unique pieces.

Elemental Cabinet, 2017

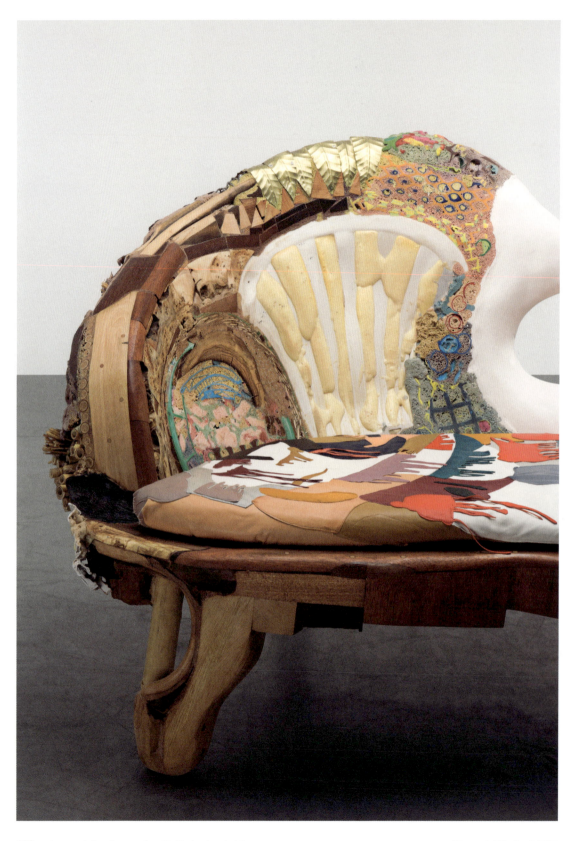

Lambridis calls himself a clumsy perfectionist, trained by trial and error, by breaking and building, and possessing a desire to fix things since childhood. The satisfaction he derives from mending and sampling is the motor of his curiosity, understanding how things are made and why different elements might yield to one another. The randomness of his approach immediately catches people's attention by reversing roles and subverting materials. As much an artist as a designer, he trespasses the borders between these two domains and creates iconoclastic hybrids that are difficult to categorize, bridging diverse fields, such as sustainability and sensationalism. He has reached for the stars since graduating at the Design Academy Eindhoven and thinks in bold and beautiful volumes.

Greek by birth, he is naturally drawn to the past where he collects fragments of materials and studies philosophy and archaeology; all transcribed into his passion for furniture design history. He assembles high and low, valuable and worthless, cultural and kitsch. When merging such materials, he anticipates the outcome ahead of time and steers design towards its own chaotic direction, overcoming the fear of failure and gaining confidence while his eclectic mix starts to develop a haphazard mind of its own.

A CONTEMPORARY COLLAGE
Kostas Lambridis

Elemental Cabinet, 2017

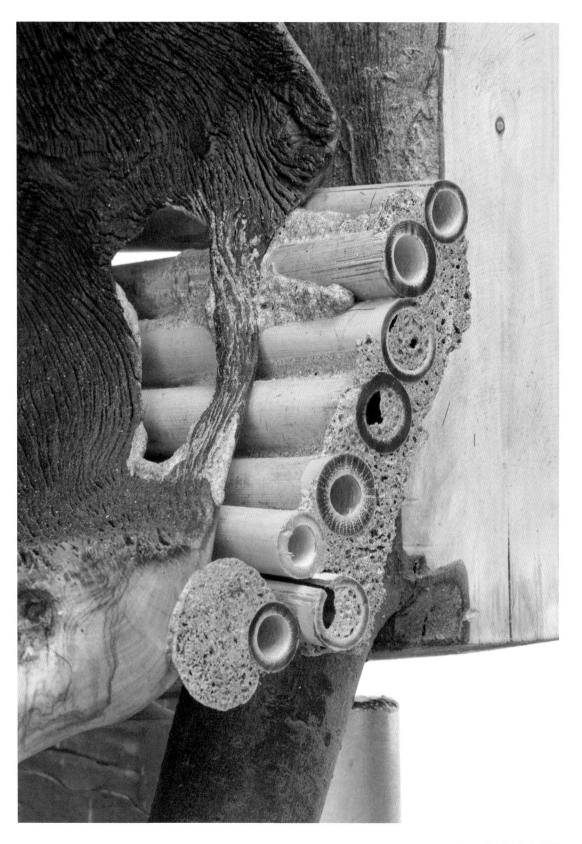

Elemental Cabinet, 2017

Elemental Cabinet, 2017

The workshop of Paul Heijnen is a wonderland of girders, hinges, screws and bolts. Like a lifesize Meccano set or giant puzzle, his meticulously-crafted furniture is slowly assembled in limited numbers and unique editions. Dig deeper and his phantasmagorical sketches reveal a complex architectural underworld – part oilrig, part tree house – multiple starting points that are constructed with the same attention to detail as a 17th century marquetry cabinet.

Heijnen's wooden furniture is built from intricate and modular pieces of oak, cedar and beech. Their Cathedral-like complexity leaves one wondering how exactly they're made – they seemingly grow in and out of one another, revealing inner workings, exposing structural skeletons and displaying symmetrical scaffolding. A cube becomes a box and then an octagon, sometimes even growing stilts as legs such as in the case of Heijnen's iconic *Hyperion* lamp.

Rounded edges emerge in his *Curved Chair*, an airy framework derived from the same aesthetics of his vaulted *Muqarnas* cabinet. The latter's arm mechanisms open up to reveal geometric inlay, as grand as the finest Islamic latticework, yet again turning the inside out. Kaleidoscopic in scope while proudly illustrating the making process, his are industrial scale ideas produced on a micro-manufacturing level.

INSIDE OUT
Paul Heijnen

Muqarnas, 2019

Piet Hein Eek workshop & showroom

Thirty-five years ago a tall, young, headstrong man graduated with an upright cupboard made from discarded wooden planks, arranged in a random colour scheme, not yet knowing that these same planks would become such an important part of his destiny. He has kept on making and selling that same cupboard design until this day; it has become his signature. Decades later, the image of these recycled planks has become a successful wallpaper print that the bourgeoisie can adopt to feel connected to his zeitgeist.

From that first act of reincarnating wooden waste to his latest glass arrangements made from lampshade stock, Piet Hein Eek has dedicated his life to the discovery of potent material resources, fished out from the slipstream of overconsumption. He uses wood but also glass, copper, metal, textiles, ceramics and more – mixing in elaborate antiques amongst his modernist showroom displays. As his practice has developed, he hired young apprentices to help him produce and gradually created a cottage industry of scale: giving work to over 30 craftsmen, 8 administrative staff members, and 30 people manning his restaurant and retail store.

The universe of Piet – as his clients, cabdrivers and colleagues affectionately call him – has become the epicentre of Eindhoven; a shopping destination and cultural institute to reckon with, furthering design's connotation to this gifted city. He holds court but is also his own jester, keeping multiple balls in the air, juggling with his ambition, enthusiasm and humanity; alternating commercial collaborations with one-of-a-kind creations, lending a helping hand to young designers along the way. He collects artefacts and curates his own curiosity cabinets. He also invites artists and designers to organize exhibitions in his space while hosting champagne parties and dinners, inviting comedians and musicians to share the podium – never a dull moment in this unique and exciting world.

Piet Hein Eek workshop

The industrial building his factory inhabits houses all this buzz, and the business has become a landmark known far beyond the borders of the Low Lands; his fame has reached outsider spaces and this is why citations of his woodwork exist all over the planet. This doesn't distract or even annoy him; he knows that being copied is the best form of flattery. On the contrary, he continues to produce the full range he has made since the beginning, creating the solid and reliable resource his furniture offers in today's fickle market. The sturdy and constructed aesthetic delivers codes of conduct such as environmental responsibility and sustaining a longer lifecycle for each product.

Over the years he has kept growing and learning, merging a keen sense of business with his innate creative insights, adding even more arrows to his bow. He designs summer cottages in France, caravans and cabins for his friends, kitchens and children's rooms for clients, and cafés for an adventurous patisserie chef. Today the last feather in his cap comes by creating a hotel on his premises, bringing permanent life to the building. A never-ending stream of activities is put into motion as seamlessly as breathing; it all seems so easy and comes so naturally. Recently he tried his hand at collaborations with other brands; and for the first time he is confronted with the demands and constraints of industrial-sized quantities, even if the products are made as craft. Yet again, he manages to create with a personal handwriting of honesty and realism inlaid with a human touch. His sense of empathy is a trademark and teaches us that products made with love contain the love long after they have left the workshop, becoming our best object and friend. At Piet Hein Eek, manufacturing gets a transcendent dimension.

THE FOUNDING FATHER
Piet Hein Eek

Piet Hein Eek showroom

Much of Peter Marigold's cabinetry exposes the raw or sawn edge – going so far as to literally split logs in two to create angles – giving a sense of archaic nobility to the humble woods he chooses. While organic in character, his philosophy is one of simplicity and soul, more akin to Shaker furniture making or the work of Japanese artisans with whom he has collaborated. Crafted in his workshop, built sturdy for the long term.

An alternative way of working wood is to apply a patina, such as in Marigold's *Bleed* cabinets that use a localised ebonising technique to stain their block-like cedar base. By employing acid to strip steel hardware of its protective zinc coating, the designer conjures a chemical reaction with the wood's tannins. The resulting bleeding effect draws attention to the woodgrain's character; creating a decorative motif that echoes the tiger striping or whiskers found in exotic lumber. In this series, Marigold is interested in exploring the bleeding boundaries around natural materials that are elevated by craft; and how these same materials are then aged by nature, returning them to their humble beginnings.

Marigold has a fine arts understanding of materials, having studied sculpture prior to design at Central Saint Martins. He listens closely to a piece of wood's features, respecting its organic curves and shapes. Duality and bi-symmetry are also recurring themes in his cleft designs. Marigold reflects on what this can reveal, "They invariably hold animal or human like characteristics, our brains are hard wired to find faces, torsos and eyes, and I enjoy this ambiguity when looking at forms created using just vegetal material."

LISTEN TO THE WOOD
Peter Marigold

Bleed, 2014

Bleed, 2014

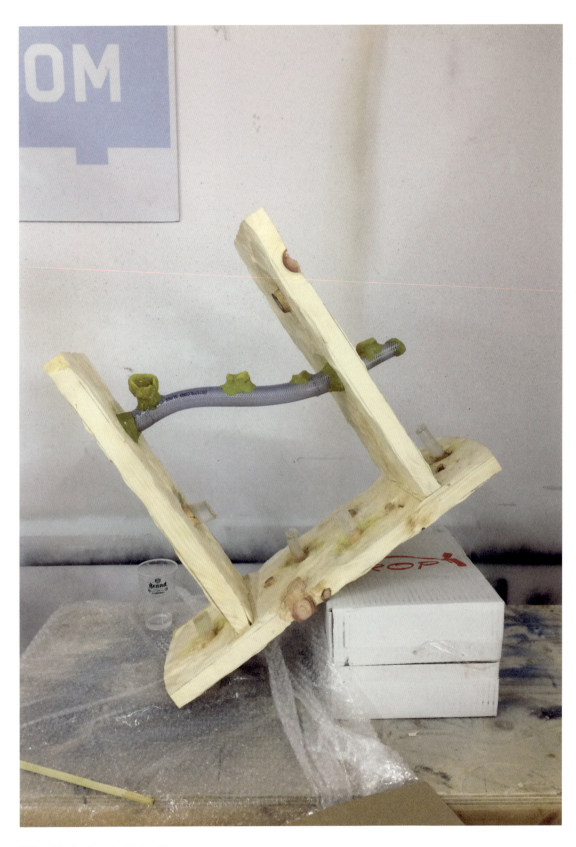

According to the Grain, 2019

Having worked as a maker of wooden furniture in his native Japan before studying at the Design Academy Eindhoven, Sho Ota has a multi-layered appreciation of natural materials; one of true respect and utter reverence. Troubled and concerned by the distance created between people and flat, uniform surfaces, the designer chisels down industrialised pine in order to return it to its natural – and more emotional – original state.

Suddenly, grains are revealed, secret knots are exposed and the positions of branches are recalled, literally bringing the user back in touch with tactile materiality and the history of the timber. An organic collection of stools, benches and tables is the result. In some cases the cut knots are even repaired by imagining the continuation of the ghost branches, albeit moulded posthumously in epoxy and beeswax.

The designer notes how trees grow wood for their own use, and not as a harvested resource for humans. Ota not only carves away at the negative aspects of a homogenized and digital world; he also uncovers the wood's undisguised structure, connecting us to the authentic essence of another living being; in this case, a tree. In *According to the Grain*, factory materials are therefore questioned and a more sustainable appreciation of nature pervades.

RETURN TO NATURE
Sho Ota

According to the Grain, 2019

According to the Grain, 2019

My Grandfather's Tree, 2009-2015

My Grandfather's Tree, 2009-2015

My Grandfather's Tree, 2009-2015

The work of Max Lamb reflects a profound respect for nature, perhaps best embodied by his intervention on a single piece of material: a towering ash tree that had been growing on his grandfather's arable land in North Yorkshire. Having climbed the great branches of this ash throughout his childhood, Lamb knew the plant's lofty limbs and soaring boughs well. Its position on the property overlooking the surrounding acres was that of a grand dame, protective of the cottage it stood beside. When the 187-year old tree's main branch died, it became apparent that it was no longer safe and that it sadly had to be felled.

Rather than simply turning it into a lifetime supply of firewood, Lamb had other plans. He contacted Jon Turnbull, a tree surgeon, to come cut it down; dissecting the great tree horizontally into 131 logs which were then dried for several years until they could be used as wood for furniture. These pieces were cut in approximately the same lengths, yet the diameter of the trunk spanned 150 centimetres at its base and just over a dowel's width at the tree's top.

Exhibited in 2015 at Somerset House in London, the cross sections were displayed on the gallery floor in the exact order of the tree, showing how all parts make one whole. Lamb had sanded and oiled the edges; a small intervention that nonetheless finished stools and tables of various sizes plus two chairs shaped by the forks of the branches – a practical niche designed by nature over time. Whereas industrial furniture erases most of the base material during the production process, in *My Grandfather's Tree, Monckton Walk Farm, 1822-2009*, Lamb listened to the wood's story and honoured all its strengths and flaws together; laid bare at the end of the tree's life, much like the trials and tribulations we encounter on the way to our own inevitable mortality.

The expression of making is at the core of Lamb's objects. For him, tools are an extension of his arms, body and mind, and the very physical act of sculpting reflects the methods he so vigorously employs. From carving and moulding to sand casting

My Grandfather's Tree, 2009–2015

and blasting, form follows process in an artisanal adaption of industrial techniques.

His earthworks come in the shape of chairs, tables, benches and stools, often carved from overburden stone, marble and granite boulders respectfully sourced as offcuts in different places. An obsession with research and exploration has therefore taken Lamb around the world, from visiting the granite quarries of Hebei Province in China to hiking along the rocky riverbanks of Mount Adamello in Italy where Tonalite is found. Being at one with both the landscape and the materials he chooses reflects veneration for nature in each of his pieces.

In *Man, Rock, Drill*, piercing and boring take on monumental proportions. By making a core drill portable, the designer was able to create works from Danby marble onsite in Vermont. Rather than sawing the slabs, Lamb used the drill to excavate his shapes. In the collection, grooves chiselled away cavities for seating and hallowed out textures to decorate stools while core cylinders became thick table legs.

Lamb also uses diamond-cutting machinery whenever a smooth surface is desired; the fewer number of cuts the better when he renders boulders into furniture. This is often combined with hand-carving to give the pieces their unique sculpted character, such as in the *De Lank* granite furniture made in his native Cornwall, or when using Delaware bluestone in the United States. The chunky chairs and stools are sometimes formulated from two boulders, meaning that Lamb has searched for pieces that snuggly fit into one another when sourcing his materials in the Catskill Mountains.

AN ODE TO MATERIALS
Max Lamb

198 Carving Stone ☛ Max Lamb

Boulders, 2017

Many designers today investigate the essence of materials to communicate more value and appreciation for our natural resources. Lex Pott has spent over ten years exploring the origins of wood, metals and stone. From oxidising different alloys to sandblasting wood grain, the Rotterdam-based designer illustrates the patina of time and evokes the rawness of things. Fascinated by the way stone roughly fractures during extraction, and how this is a stark contrast to the flatness of processed surfaces, when Pott goes to the quarry he is looking at the beauty of broken fragments that can be transformed into long-lasting furniture. Often these custom-made pieces are cut from a single slab.

Stone & Industry Table, 2009

Belgian bluestone is usually processed into rectangular blocks or plates; however Pott seeks to respect the rock's innate formations that are fundamentally rugged while also referencing its industrial use. This primal matter becomes a robust table that maintains nature's core while juxtaposing the smooth mechanical cutting of manufacturing. A hybrid example of organic-industrial, two normally opposed notions that will become more important when embedding design's future with soul.

BETWEEN STONE & INDUSTRY
Lex Pott

For centuries, ruins were pillared to construct lasting monuments to the gods and higher powers. The sites were considered contemporary quarries where it was cheap and easy to mine building materials for new architecture. Today a research project initiated by Brandon Clifford at MIT's Matter Design department is doing exactly the same thing for a new age: saving the unparalleled amount of massive concrete debris found in American landfills. The mythical method from the past known as cyclopean masonry is translated into a contemporary digital process, where elements are precisely connected, despite their diverse shapes and textures. This heroic feat conjures up the legends of giants; a full-scale architectural ode to urban decay, built using the demolition waste that is gathered, scanned and processed through an intuitive algorithmic flow.

Before assembly, the surface of each piece of industrial rock is carved by a robot to give it form and structure. The prototype merges ancient manufacturing principles with digital design methods, proposing material cannibalism as a means of absorbing excessive urban building residue; architectural edifices that digest themselves to create our cities of the future. The project is also detailed in a limited edition recipe book titled *The Cannibal's Cookbook: Mining Myths of Cyclopean Constructions*.

CYCLOPEAN CONSTRUCTIONS
Matter Design / MIT

Cyclopean Cannibalism, 2017

206 Carving Stone 🖝 Matter Design / MIT

Cyclopean Cannibalism, 2017

Cyclopean Cannibalism, 2017

In Hale, 2020

Marble is one of nature's most appreciated gifts, its remarkable veining and colours have been revered for centuries. In order to reduce the impact on quarries, conscious designers nowadays use overburden and discards instead. Part stonemason, part sculptor, Ben Storms is one such creative. By literally putting leftover material on a pedestal to make limited edition tables and benches, the Belgian allows the marble's sculptural beauty to be admired without excessive detriment to the environment.

The blocks are polished on one side while leaving their underside raw, reminding the collector of the stone's natural origins and that it is not industrial despite its smoothened appearance. Storms positions the marble on a three-dimensional pillow made by inflating two pieces of sheet metal; a stainless, copper or gold brass base that magically elevates the cherished surface on a cushion of air. Storms named this series *In Hale*. The inverse is expressed in *Ex Hale*, when the inflated shape is 3D scanned before being sculpted on a CNC milling machine out of a single slab of marble. Storms' works therefore play with the soft and hard aspects of air, alloy and stone while revealing the alchemistic properties of materials.

ELEVATING MATERIALS
Ben Storms

Ex Hale, 2020

The industrial process of cast moulding is at the core of French-born designer Martin Laforet's work. Graduating from the Design Academy Eindhoven – also the city where he has established his practice – he produces unique editions of robust objects and furniture. By incorporating the original moulds directly into his pieces, he contemplates the limitations of being a young designer today.

In *Mould Objects*, Laforet investigates the transition of materials such as concrete and bronze. Oak moulds and casts are strapped and stacked together; a make-do aesthetic that is balanced and sophisticated despite its rudimentary essence. By taking the mould out of its industrial context and bringing it into a domestic interior, the designer explores the notions of cohabitation and contrast. A low circular coffee table suggests the centre of a nomadic campsite. A lamp is improvised out of a brick and an elongated rebar. Chairs are assembled from inversed casts and their wooden mould; the oak imprinting its organic grain onto the surface. The bronze tops of side tables are stamped onto their concrete bases, forging a sturdy factory seal. Laforet's fabrications therefore exist at the intersection of sculpture, industry and architecture. His combines seem like found archaeological artefacts yet his amalgamating approach to materials leaves its mark on the future.

THE IMPRINT OF TIME
Martin Laforet

MCCT1, 2019

MCV2, 2019

MCT1, 2019

MCT2, 2019

Archaeology is the study of human life and customs through excavations and the analysis of material fragments; it therefore consists of remnants from ancient artefacts and architecture that define the cultural landscape of the historic past. As one of the humanities, this social science is related to anthropology, and has various outcomes that range from reconstructing the ways people lived to decrypting social and political changes in civilisation.

In Paul Cockedge's case, however, it uncovers an archaeology of the present; one where excavations pay witness to contemporary architecture, geography, geology, sociology and social criticism. 2017's *Excavation: Evicted* is a poignant reminder of how the free market and capital greed have forced artists and designers out of the centres of major cities. Cocksedge was notified he was going to be expelled from his London studio to make way for more luxury apartments, often bought by foreigners that would possibly never even live there. His response transformed into a form of activism when

Excavation: Evicted, 2017

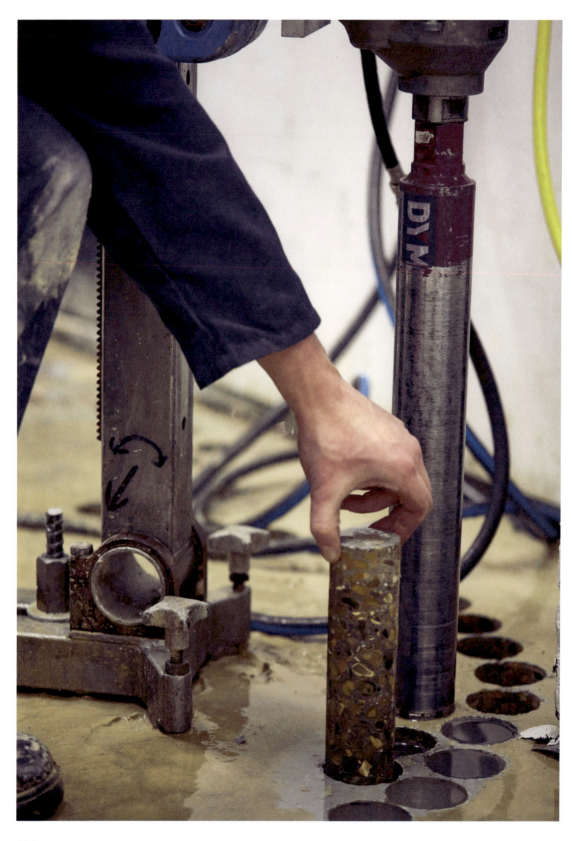

Excavation: Evicted, 2017

he decided to scavenge for material mementos of his own time there and the life of the building itself. He started drilling into the basement floor and extracted several tonnes of material in its very foundations; a form of urban mining, destined to become an aesthetic critique through design. The extracted cylinders contained modern concrete and historical bricks from the site's former existence as a stable; these were sanded and polished into multiple elements to build a new collection of furniture. The series of autonomous design objects combined the coarse concrete with light and transparent glass, to expose the unexpected internal terrazzo patterns of the recovered materials, and to fully highlight the weight of the social issue at hand. In a cynical coincidence of his actions, the renowned series was subsequently collected by wealthy collectors – illustrating that creative genius is able to fight eviction with cultural conviction.

ARCHAEOLOGY OF THE PRESENT
Paul Cocksedge

Excavating Fragments 🖝 Paul Cocksedge

Excavation: Evicted, 2017

Her world is one that rejects the status quo, opting for change in a most radical way. As a researcher and dreamer, Zoe Joe Rae tackles our abundance of waste, the loss of resourcefulness due to technology and the threat to cultures from standardization. Formulating answers for an obsolete way of living, jeopardized by global warming and viral threats. Like an imaginary hunter-gatherer, she traces the beginning of human life and culture, and incorporates the initial processes of making, fishing, walking and boating. She has meticulously studied indigenous life to abstract its positive aspects in order to preserve them for the future, initiating innovative techniques that are age-old and brand new at the same time – reinvented for our age.

Joe Rae hunts for materials such as plastic milk bottles to create the layered skin of her kayak and the material for her paddles, and gathers multiple stacks of coffee packaging and egg boxes to transform into protective forms of clothing and travel bags. Her catch requires being in the right place at the right time to find the maximum amount of ingredients before they are sent off to recycling centres. She uses each scrap and nothing is discarded as a matter

Hunter Gatherer in the Anthropocene, 2017

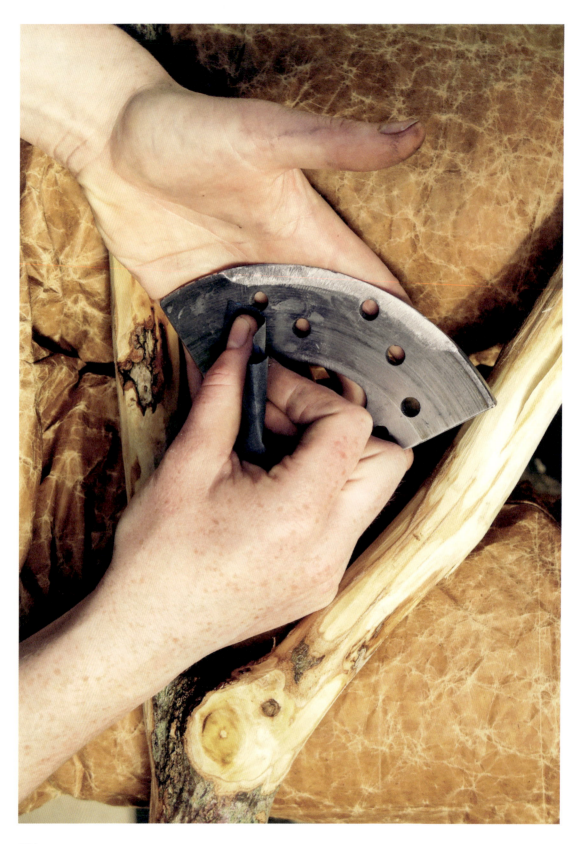

Hunter Gatherer in the Anthropocene, 2017

of principle. Fighting against the homogenous way our products are made, the wild designer proposes an alternative vocabulary for her pieces, playing out the part to the fullest.

Like an archaeologist, she divides her quests into several chapters, discovering varying answers to the different challenges of making materials and forming shapes. Used for the study and exploration of new waterways, the kayak is a vehicle that harks back to ancient times while also relating to contemporary life. Using the milk bottles as a herd, she skins her animals to make the hermetic plastic cover of her kayak, which is constructed and crafted by hand from sycamore saplings, a renewable resource. The paddles are moulded in wood from preheated plastics, and her clothes are composed from paper and cardboard packaging. Rethinking design and production techniques illustrates how indigenous cultures may help us to survive. The inclusion of animal icons and handcrafted tools in the collection of artefacts furthers her ideas as touching and intrinsically human.

HUNTER & GATHERER
Zoe Joe Rae

Hunter Gatherer in the Anthropocene, 2017

Hunter Gatherer in the Anthropocene, 2017

As an award-winning solar designer, Marjan van Aubel's innovative practice spans the fields of sustainability, design and technology. James Shaw's autonomous work questions the materials and methods involved in the creation of objects. Both of them have high esteem for resources at a time when it has become clear that we can no longer continue to pillage the earth's reserves; challenging the notion of how waste materials should be appreciated and embedded with more value. No feat is too large or small to address, from Shaw's recycled HDPE furniture to van Aubel's solar panel design for the roof of the Dutch Pavilion at the Dubai World Expo in 2021.

The pair was troubled by the fact that industrial wood processing produces a staggering 50% to 80% of timber wastage. They collaborated to study methods of incorporating waste shavings into the production of a bio-resin. A lightweight, mushy and mouldable material was created, foaming up and expanding multiple times when the resin came into contact with the various textures of the shaving fibres. The reinforced compound mixture was then hand-sculpted into the underside of a chair mould and its four ash legs, setting into shape and exposing a rough back edge – a serial product that remains unique each time because of this action-packing process.

Well Proven Chair is the outcome; one of the first furniture pieces to be assessed with Life Cycle Analysis (LCA), evaluating its total environmental impact throughout its production and usage. Accompanied by stools in various heights and a chaise longue, the designers' pulpy collection comes in a neutral range of earthy dyed colours.

MALLEABLE MATTERS
Marjan van Aubel & James Shaw

Well Proven Chair, 2012

Paperpulp Cabinet, 2009

A circular philosophy has always been a constant in Debbie Wijskamp's design career. Her approach to incorporating upcycling is one that gives an organic essence back to the source ingredient. Since graduating from Arnhem's ArtEZ academy in 2009, she has dedicated herself to producing a vast body of *Paperpulp* works, mainly vases and table accessories made from compressing recycled paper and water-based binders.

In the case of newspaper and waste paper, her coarse containers are cast as millennial shapes reminiscent of archeological vessels for food and water. Equally inspired by the improvised nature of furniture in distant cultures, and wanting to create her own building material, she designed the *Paperpulp Cabinet* series. These rudimentary stacks of boxes, crates and drawers are archaic in spirit yet industrial in technique.

Pigment brings a vibrant additional layer to Wijskamp's collections, as does the introduction of salt crystals to the surfaces of products and wall objects, embedding the humble pulp with a twinkling energy. The ancient character of her pieces is not accidental; the rounded abstract forms seem to have a life of their own – or indeed belong to a fictitious tribal community.

A FAMILY OF FORM
Debbie Wijskamp

Paperpulp Collectibles, 2017

Llegado, 2018

Throughout his prolific career, Taeg Nishimoto has been in dialogue with fibre, form and space; a lifelong study of materials and shapes that have the power to reconcile with nature in the urban environment. His architectural practice is nomadic, following him from his native Japan to Amsterdam and then Cornell University to complete a masters in architecture, as well as distinguished campuses across the United States where he has since taught. As a designer, he has created installations, lighting, vases and furniture, fracturing and furrowing the surface to reveal the organic essence of things.

His understanding of nature is evidenced when contemplating how paper begins life as a sapling before growing into a resilient tree. Although transformed into relatively fragile thin sheets of paper, Nishimoto wanted to give the material its strength back with the creation of *Llegado*; a stool made from recycled paper.

The pulp is wet felted and moulded into an essential and almost archaic structure; given colour by the traces of ink that once covered this paper's surface. As a second texture, surplus metal shavings collected in a metalshop are added to the wet pulp to rust and create an oxidized effect, mimicking the glazing process of Raku pottery. *Llegado*'s legs are formulated around wooden rods, creating a concave void of space under each stool. Its heavy concrete-like appearance and the industrial aspect of moulding are both balanced by the artisanal felting process that is handmade and requires two weeks of slow drying.

THE ESSENCE OF THINGS
Taeg Nishimoto

Llegado, 2018

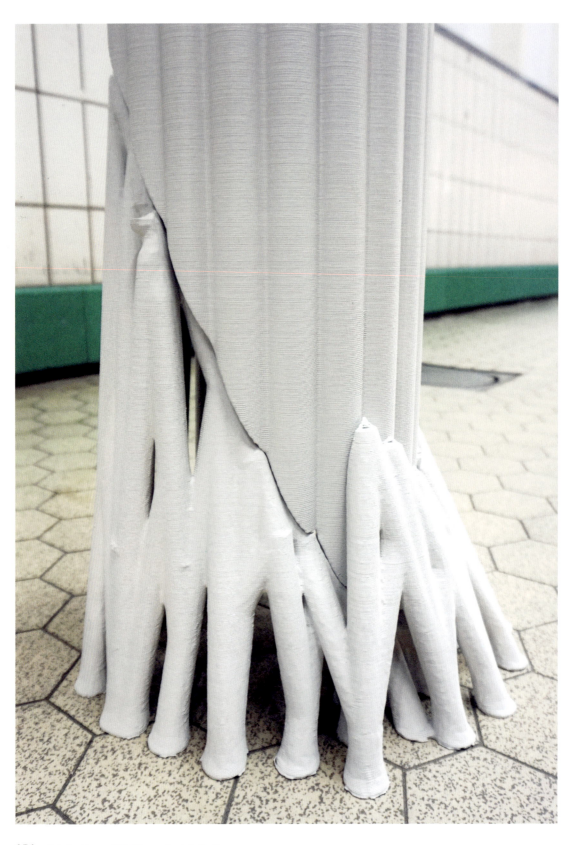

Pasta Shoota, 2019

Of all the extruded products in the world, there is none more famous than pasta. It is imbued with multiple socio-cultural meanings; existing in various forms since the 1st century and becoming a food staple, not just for Italy, but in many parts of the world. In Italy, common pasta is as representative of family gatherings as breaking bread and recalls the post-war era of industrialisation and prosperity. Regardless of how many culinary chefs elevate its more than 300 known shapes, its essence is one of democratic functionality, albeit bordering on kitsch in some circumstances.

Such was the subject of Gianmaria della Ratta's contextual design masters at the Design Academy Eindhoven. He uses contemporary software to imagine the unexpected, and in *Pasta Shootah* – a deliberately colloquial title for the most populaire of foods – he has deconstructed the carb's context by painting extrusion in a new light. Fabricated on a 3D printer, his furniture, bowls and sculptural elements are oversized tubes, reconfigured with adjoining pipes and support systems like something out of a science lab. Their oversized proportion and unfamiliar colourings quickly beguile the viewer into thinking futurism inspires them instead of the pantry. Fundamentally experimental, della Ratta's project challenges clichéd stereotypes and critiques the stagnant traditionalism in Italian design, simultaneously reversing form follows function and illustrating how future manufacturing can be as evident as the most humble of techniques. The young designer observes how his theory "Appropriates pasta as a primary source, beyond its culinary origins, to explore technology and making in a cultural context. By translating extrusion from the main method of pasta production to 3D software, new rules emerge for efficiency, form, scale, and process."

TAKEN OUT OF CONTEXT
Gianmaria della Ratta

Pasta Shoota, 2019

There is growing consensus in the design and fashion industries that paper is going to be one of the materials of a more conscious tomorrow. Beer Holthuis is someone who believes in this revolution. Alarmed by the large amounts of paper humans waste every year – a staggering 80 kilograms on average for each of us – he has developed the world's first 3D printer that is able to print recycled paper pulp. The circular possibilities offered by paper objects are as endless, as the number of generations such products can exist.

The printed matter is surprisingly durable, using a natural binder to create the composite. Holthuis has embraced the slubby and tactile qualities of the material in his initial designs for lamps, vessels and vases. The pulp is slowly printed out in a coiling movement, rendering his organically-shaped objects with bold gusto; instinctively leading him to conical forms reminiscent of seashells or petrified fossils. Grown in different shades of grey, the newsprint lends its recognizable complexion to the designer's creations, although the items could of course embody the original hues of any type of paper. Made to order, this sustainable production system abolishes the need for large stockpiles, absorbs a readily available waste resource, and can reduce the need for long-distance transport since manufacturing can take place locally. What was seen as utopian even a decade ago now turns out to be a rather simple and evident solution for manufacturing the artefacts and packaging of the future.

A PAPER REVOLUTION
Beer Holthuis

Paper Pulp Printer, 2020

I Dream of Megalithic Times, 2019

Designers sometimes turn to prehistoric inspirations when creating objects for the future. Like a contemporary Fred or Wilma Flintstone, they excavate pebbles, rocks and canyons into design and architecture, organically shaping space around us. Elissa Lacoste follows this path to finding primitive form; "dreaming of megalithic times" to quote the title of her collection.

The French-based designer's work seems at first to be of mineral origin however on closer inspection, her archaeological furniture is soft and round, pigmented in strange tones and possessing a smooth silicone surface. Tamed for the interior rather than blending in, these rugged speleothems double as chairs, tables, stools and desks. Made from natural-based putty and paste, they are sculpted directly onto wire frames and structures before being sanded for practicality in sections such as tabletops and seats. Partly inspired by the photography of planetary terrains, these alien troglodyte pieces could have slowly evolved over millennia. They surprise and provoke the sensorial experience of any visitor or user.

OTHERWORLDLY FORMS
Elissa Lacoste

Dolomies, 2019

I Dream of Megalithic Times, 2019

They awake from their nap into a dreamscape that's imagined but not regulated from deep within the subconscious. Yuko Nishikawa describes the tension in her work as *pikupiku*, a Japanese term that can mean something uncontrollable yet surprising – like the inadvertent twitch of a sleeping deer's ear. Her joyful clay characters definitely have a soul of their own, tickling the sensations of the collector. Globular forms shaped by hand that inflate like bubbles; some of them have openings, others grow legs, hands or horns. A lively and unexpected vocabulary, akin to the notion of organic surrealism.

The designer's ceramics come in subdued pastel shades, patinaed tactile surfaces ranging from putty and matcha to purple, lapis and terracotta; powdery yet always possessing a radioactive glow. Cut-out circles and balls introduce a narrative accent. Lamps and chandeliers formulate orbiting satellites sent into space from the Stone Age. Sculptures and vases seem like earthen seedpods that have been blown up and morphed into something else. These rounded objects are conical and drawn from nature's past while previewing its future. Nishikawa's creations grow in the Brooklyn studio she has appropriately dubbed *the forest*; post-fossil, post-organic, post-pandemic.

POST-FOSSIL
Yuko Nishikawa

Time Vessels Collection, 2017

Time Vessels Collection, 2017

Technology is often seen as a barrier between craftsmanship and the handmade. *Adaptive Manufacturing* is an on-going collaboration between Olivier van Herpt and Sander Wassink that revaluates that theory. By using a 3D printer to create and throw ceramics in a new way, the duo investigate how technology is replacing the handcrafted while inventing an industrial production process. The designers ask, "What if our machines could become more sensory? What if the machine could sense the local environment and incorporate it into the production process?"

To illustrate this notion, they programmed a printer to be affected by external factors, such as vibrations and sound waves. These pulsations and tiny tremors document a specific site and moment in time; measured by sensors that translate these currents into the organic forms of vases and ceramic totems. That which resembles a carved piece of wood, a woven wicker basket, a hornet's hive, termite mound or geological

Adaptive Manufacturing, 2014–present

fossil, is in fact crafted from the most contemporary of technologies.

The objects are printed in clay over a series of days. Yet the designers see the mechanised technology as an extension of their artisan minds and hands; still in control of its actions whilst leaving its layered strata up to chance, formulated by the environment around us. As graduates of the Design Academy Eindhoven, the pair has spent the past six years experimenting with extrusion and printing techniques in natural materials such as clay and beeswax. On a much slower scale – metaphorically and quite literally – both designers strive to reintroduce the presence of the human within industrial manufacturing.

THE NEW PULSE OF MANUFACTURING
Olivier van Herpt & Sander Wassink

Adaptive Manufacturing, 2014–present

Gypsum is a mineral long used in construction and the creative arts to formulate plaster. The sulphates in its dry white powder create a chemical reaction when encountering water, producing a malleable paste that can be cast or moulded, including in the medical field to protect our repairing bones. These divergent aspects and more intrigue the designer Jeroen Wand who experiments with materials and processes, reinterpreting them in unconventional ways to innovate and develop his own techniques such as paper laminating and manual rotation moulding.

    Plaster moulding is most prevalent in *Phases*, a series of vases concocted in two stages. The object's shape is first cast and dried for two days, before

Jeroen Wand in his workshop

it is dipped in freshly mixed liquid plaster. During this process, the new plaster coats the bottle's base, slowly dripping and modifying form while freely reacting against itself. The designer's raw and unpolished aesthetic style is expressed through multiple immersions that create a rough palette of textures and accidental surfaces. Pigment is added directly into each batch of the plaster, giving the improvised and irregular layers a subtle hue. Serially produced in different sizes yet entirely artisanal by technique, Wand's designs express the conflict between two entities of the same origin while calming the eye with a still life presence.

LAYERED TEXTURES
Jeroen Wand

Phases, 2012-2016

Floris Wubben in his workshop

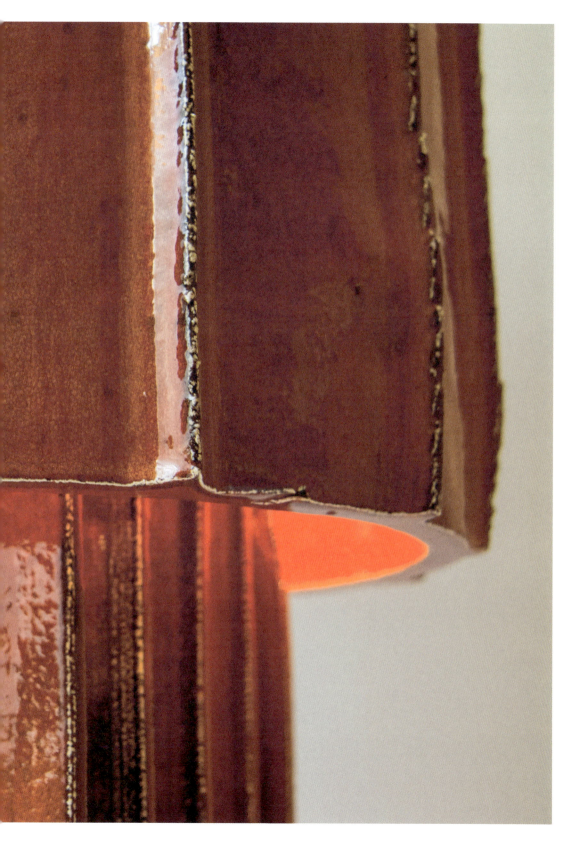

Saw Lamp, 2019

Is it possible to merge nature, craft and industry into one design concept? Floris Wubben has been working along these lines ever since conceiving a bench that combined the delicate pleating of a white polypropylene "textile" with the presence of burly wooden branches as legs. Here, synthetic and organic needed one another to stabilize and survive; a poetic balancing act that reflects the designer's methodology, pivoting the hand of the maker against the innate beauty of natural materials.

In recent years, Wubben's practice has evolved into the creation of low-tech machines that become part of the design process. His material of choice is clay, using extrusion techniques to forge uniquely-shaped serial pieces. What started with the best-selling *Pressed* vases quickly evolved into applying similar techniques to the making of ceramic lamps, chairs and tables. In his *Pressed* collection and *Hammered Bowls*, objects possess a distinctly physical quality, yet instead of coming from a sculptor's studio, they are crafted by hand in the workshop. By guiding the profiles of the extruded forms, variations in three-dimensional grooves and furrows are made possible across the surface. The pieces are robust and express the heavy-duty manual interventions needed to extrude them: pushed into decorative contours through the press or hammered with a large mallet to create organic rings with each hefty belt. Any resulting lumps or cracks in the material all form part of the sprouting process. Whether tinted with thick glazes or simply coloured by natural patina, finish is another area of exploration; including the use of live flames to etch texture into unbaked porcelain, mimicking the erosion of landscape on a micro level. The feat of throwing Wubben's ceramics is thus reinvented by mechanical devices, manpower and a creative imagination.

EXTRUSION & EROSION
Floris Wubben

"When primal instincts, desires, emotions and fears rise from the bottom of our subconscious to the forefront of our awareness, we are forced to reconcile our waking consciousness in the material world with the primal elements that make us human". Thus observes the American-born Eindhoven-based designer Carlo Lorenzetti. Like many of his generation, he is concerned by the alienation society is experiencing; perhaps now more than ever. Alienation from the familiar, the banal, the analogue, the real – and each other of course.

In order to regain our lost footing, he proposes a solid body of grounding objects that reconnect us to touch, sound, sight and even smell. By creating archetypal clay vessels and oversized tools that hark back to essential function and primitive form, he single-handedly transports us to a parallel universe where profound questions can be asked. Delving into our subconscious and possibly ancestral experiences, refamiliarising us with the vocabulary and gestures that make us intrinsically human.

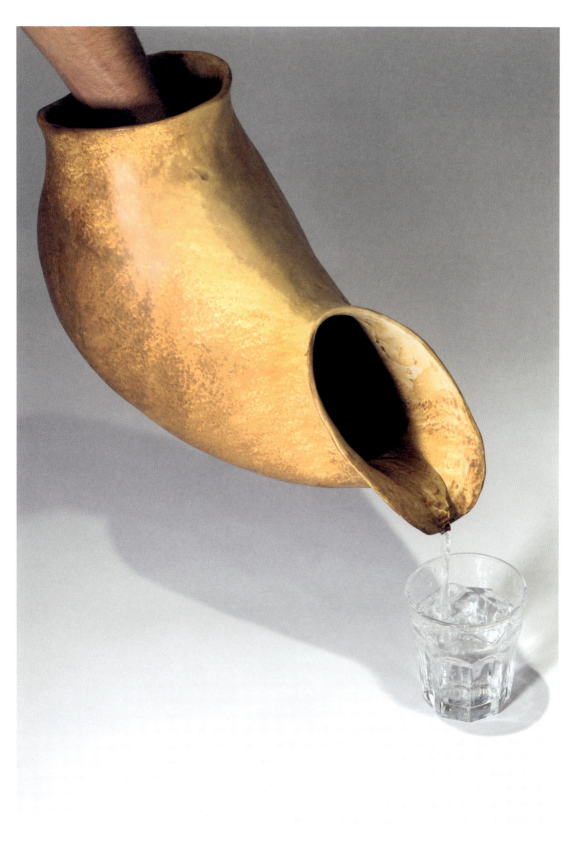

Carafe, 2015

USB Charger, 2015

This anthromorphic quest begins with a milk-glazed water carafe that invites us to intuitively pour it, provoking the user to address the complexities of their own body. His *Earhorn* is an elongated conical apparatus that opens up an intimate channel of communication between two people. Another body extension facilitates the collecting of water from a well. His *Censer* burns incense to pervade any modern ritual, composed of two chambers that gently vibrate with kinetic energy. He also created the *Flywheel*, a mechanical device with a USB port that indolently generates energy by the spinning of a large clay wheel; an action that resets our notion of technology by truly understanding what is needed to power it. These artefacts are all large, requiring heavy lifting and the full use of the body. By sculpting a material made from the brown earth, Lorenzetti literally puts nature in our grasp.

ANCESTRAL ARCHETYPES
Carlo Lorenzetti

USB Charger, 2015

As a post-Palaeolithic creator, Nacho Carbonell can be seen as a contemporary designer who makes drawings like cave paintings, animals like sculptures and chairs like dwellings. Exactly as in the art of that period, he divides his design into two categories – the figurative part that depicts beasts and household objects, and the non-figurative, which consists of organic shapes and ritual symbols. Like a Stone-Age figure, he digs for sand which is then packaged in latex skins, breaking glass shards to act as aggressive armour, whilst inventing vegetal fibre and shaggy sheepskins, pretending they are the hides of wild animals roaring with animistic energy.

 His materials create an interaction with the audience, an almost physical link between the object and its observer. They cause people to dream and to use their senses. This materialisation helps the designer engage the user with the work, fusing them into a single experience. Today, a new strain of thinking in philosophy states that materials will acquire a new status, where they prevail and are able to connect on their own terms. Evidently the process of materialisation is becoming an important idiom and we must pay homage to these primal principles at work.

Metal Rug: Steel, 2016

For Carbonell, materials are liquefied so that they can be sprayed onto floating mesh structures, amalgamated with combinations of sand and silicone, paper and pigment, sawdust with glue. The studio reinvents and adapts tools to be able to spray these magic concoctions that are akin to shamanic potions. His one-of-a-kind hand-knit rugs for Nodus are an extension of such material magic. Produced in Nepal, their loops each weave the alloys of aluminium, steel, brass and copper into circular moons of alchemic power.

Carbonell's materials embrace, always maintaining direct contact with the hands, creating an organic language from bodily involvement, and immersing us in a one-on-one experience with the work, so that, through the process of contemplation, we become one with the archaic token. With his unruly dreadlocks, deep voice, dancing gait and agile movements, Carbonell seems a lot like a modern-day caveman, he resembles one of the first ever humans who created craft and culture, the so-called Homo Habilis.

THE RITUAL OF MAKING
Nacho Carbonell

Metal Rug: Brass, 2016

Radical Fossils, 2016

Radical Fossils, 2016

A contemporary form of alchemy is present in the monolithic works of Hongjie Yang. The Eindhoven-based artist and designer experiments with casting techniques, merging artisanal methods with new advances, machine polishing and finishing. The result is a transformation of materials and an evolution of patina; a vocabulary for the future which simultaneously speaks of archaeology, geology and technology, bridging the dichotomy between nature and manufacturing.

When making his *Radical Fossils*, Yang combines alloys such as aluminium, bronze and brass with ceramics. The extreme texture of the oxidised forms and molten matter is contrasted by surfaces so highly polished that they can act as mirrors. Primitive in their aspect yet industrial to the core, Yang's furniture and sculpture blurs the distinctions between his materials' mineral origin and their rough manmade appearance. In less abstract works, aluminium, zinc and stainless steel are cast into the shapes of a log or decorative branch; the permanence of time conflicting with the transient complexities of modern society. Other projects include collaborating with biomedical engineers to add human tissue to 3D-printed Delftware; a further step in questioning the presence of technology in the craft and design continuum.

MONOLITHIC ALCHEMY
Hongjie Yang

Radical Fossils, 2016

Weldgrown, 2017

Throughout his career, Tomáš Libertíny has fluttered – or should one say buzzed? – between the blurry frontiers of art and design. Yet leaving these two autonomous spheres aside, his work more importantly celebrates the beauty of nature and the complexities of the human spirit. His background in engineering compliments his talent for sculpture, painting and conceptual design processes. Technology and machinery are kept at bay; controlled, a means to an end as he puts it, providing a pragmatic framework within which the organic can prosper and the presence of the hand is felt.

The making techniques he employs are multiple, ranging from the poetic and fragile to the heavy duty, or even combining the two. Crafted using stainless steel, beeswax and a welding machine that slowly grows circular formations over a period of two weeks, *Weldgrown* is a large recipient that embodies Libertíny's continued use of slow processes in his interventions. From using a ballpoint pen to saturate an entire maple cupboard in blue to collaborating with bees to turn honeycomb into a biophilic urn or vase, the Slovakian artist illustrates how design's future will be about patience and the growing of materials and form.

WELDED MARVEL
Tomáš Libertíny

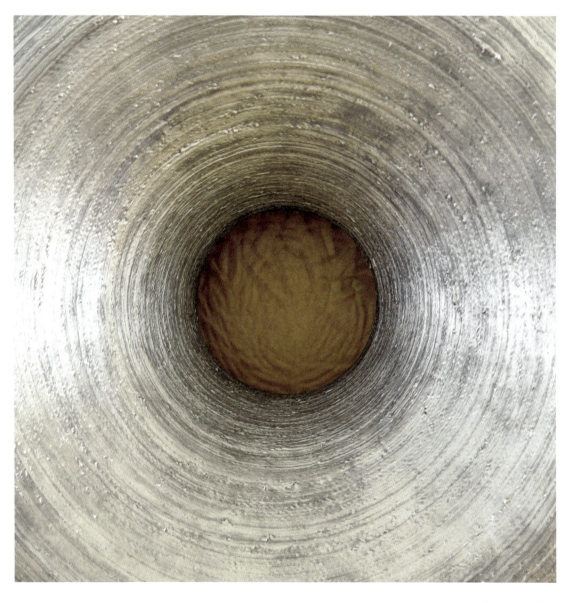

Weldgrown, 2017

Micro Urban Mining, 2015

One of the environment's most encroaching problems is the massive stream of e-waste being generated each day. Our insatiable appetite for technology mixed with planned obsolescence and an out-dated consumer culture that promotes newness, mean that more than 50 million metric tonnes of electronics are discarded annually; so great that the U.N. called it a "tsunami" in 2019. Several designers are addressing the issue through urban mining; the collecting and recycling of the valuable metals found in these throwaways, inspiring reflection on how design and advanced thinking can become part of the solution. A three-year study called *Ore Streams* by Formafantasma reported that by 2080 there will be more mineral reserves above ground than below; an unimaginable reality that proves we need to start mining the waste we already have.

Jorien Wiltenburg has been investigating the vast sums of money being spent on recycling our metals and the lack of knowledge consumers have about what they are dumping; for example, more than $60 million of gold and silver are tossed out each year alone. The majority of e-waste ends up in landfill in developing countries, poisoning the soil with its toxins while also being toxic to the lives of the disadvantaged sorters and scavengers. Through her project and an accompanying film, Wiltenburg wishes to alter our perceptions and consciousness. This small-scale example of micro extraction can become a worldwide manufacturing system if we only would try. "Restoring the connections between creating and using an object" as she says.

URBAN MINING
Jorien Wiltenburg

Tafla, 2012

He takes things apart in order to scrutinize their inner systems. He loves the mechanical and the robotic, asking technology to lend a helping hand when crafting his unique objects. Oskar Zieta's world is one of organised obsession. Obsessed by the lightness of being. As a true industrial designer, he venerates classic materials such as steel, without accepting its constraints and weight. He seeks to change the metal's robust image and therefore designs new processes, reinventing the massive matter by making it lighter, frivolous and reflective. He welded two thin layers of metal at the edges to make a chamber; able to be expanded by pumping up its cavity. Thus he achieved his dream of playful elements called *Plopp*.

The main goal of his studio is to introduce customization to design while keeping production, transport and storage as efficient as in manufactured objects. This meeting of the industrial and the unique creates a product line that visually corresponds to the two domains, blending them into one cutting edge language of bold abstract fragments in steel; durable structures produced on demand.

The latest instalments in the collection are about rediscovering the idea of metallic mirrors, just like the first examples found on earth. The stretched steel gives a slightly distorted shape to the mirrors, which are blown up and bent a bit at the ends, transforming these designs into reflective surfaces that slightly twist perception. The resulting ovals meditate upon a surreal world of wonder that positions itself between man and machine, brain and robot, the unique and the serial.

ORGANISED OBSESSION
Oskar Zieta

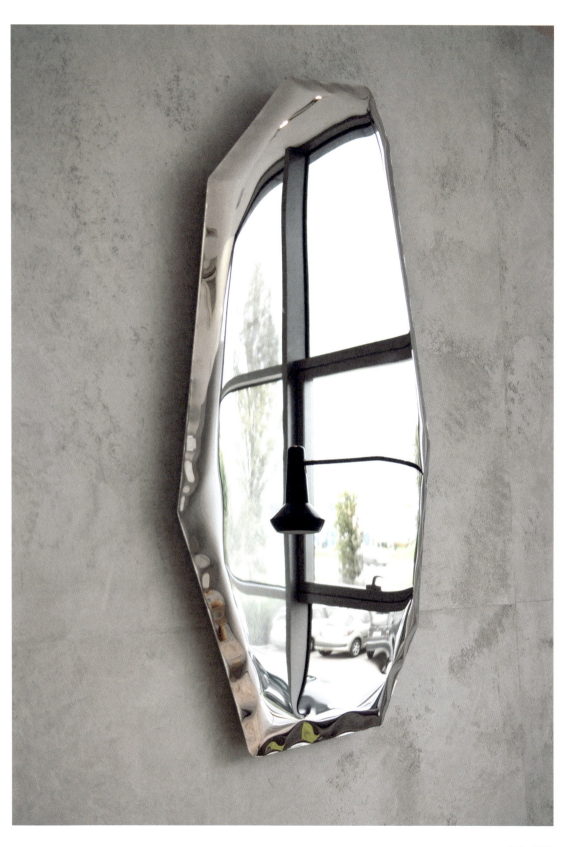

Tafla, 2012

Pewter has had a long history of use from the Bronze Age to Egypt to the countless tankards that fill antique stores today. The alloy is mainly composed of tin, an increasingly rare extracted resource that should not be thrown away. Rutger de Regt decided to recycle existing pewter items by casting a stool that combines a strict slender mould with a swirling pouring technique; alluding to the metal's liquid properties when heated and featuring impossibly thin legs. The molten material is applied in three stages, with the second and third layers chemically reacting to the previous one, generating a lively organic texture. Forging shape out of thin air, one step at a time; like drawing in three-dimensional space or the rocky sediments in minerals and stone that evolve over time.

As a process-based designer, de Regt incorporates industrial techniques on a sustainable scale, creating a dialogue between materials and production methods. With a passion for experimentation and composite thinking, he heads the HandMade Industrials studio in collaboration with co-founder Marlies van Putten. Their aesthetic style gives chunky form to globular vases and plump furniture.

MOLTEN MOULDING
Rutger de Regt

Make & Mold Pewter, 2012

The idea of infusing an object with soul is poetically expressed in the glasswork of Philipp Weber. The Berlin-based designer is one of many who honour the craft processes that are increasingly rare in our digitized world. By hacking the glassblowing windpipe and adding keys, he introduces a new dimension to the relationship between the glassmith and their creation.

Weber's contemporary instrument is indeed musical, permitting the craftsperson to alter the piece's air chambers by pressing on the valves and improvising form. Thus the two thousand year-old technique of blowing glass is given new life. Weber says he is forging an allegoric bond of craft and music. A melodic cacophony fills the sweltering blower's studio; molten magic taking shape while flames fly in between the furnaces.

The designer is intrigued by the alchemy of creating glass and the drama of composing sound, merging these transient movements together. He captured this interaction during a live performance at the Nationaal Glasmuseum in Leerdam in 2015 – collaborating with master blowers Christop Genard and Emil Kovac alongside renowned cellist Ernst Reijseger – an interdisciplinary post-Fluxus moment, reflecting an energy much like the dynamism of jamming musicians. Weber has since applied shots of colour to his refracting glass pieces and further investigated the arts with a collection of hanging lamps, their blown volumes inspired by the movements of dance.

ACQUIRED ENERGY
Philipp Weber

A Strange Symphony, 2013

A Strange Symphony, 2013

Basket Stool, 2018

Arnout Visser has dedicated his design career to glass, having discovered its resilient properties and beauty in the 1990s when he created some of Droog's most memorable pieces. These sober items were a far cry from the more flamboyant schooling he received at the Domus Academy where he studied under Memphis greats such as Sottsass, de Lucchi and Mendini. And yet his work today is a delightful mix of the two approaches: iconic yet industrial, playful yet pragmatic.

Visser has innovated a unique technique he calls lost basket, in reference to the lost wax casting process that has been used for six millennia. Glass is fired to 700 degrees when it is malleable enough to fill the intertwining grooves of a woven wicker basket. While the water-soaked cane quickly dissolves, burnt away by the heat of the molten material, the basketweave leaves its imprint on the piece. Gradually cooling down under controlled conditions, this roughened material is then sawed, cut and polished. The result is a durable glass stool that is strong enough to sit on. Visser has developed a range of alloy colours that are applied to the inside of the stools, while others are kept transparent – a rustic representation of a void, giving craft a decorative yet ghostly presence.

CASTING CRAFT
Arnout Visser

Basket Stool, 2018

Eiaculatum, 2009

Towards the end of his graphic design career, his work became more seasoned and less direct, playing with transparency and fluidity to form a remarkable ABC. The *Naked Ladies Alphabet* had made Anthon Beeke world famous at the end of the 60s when he photographed a host of attractive young girls to give shape to a human typeface in the tradition of the illustrative letter. When photography replaced drawing, this writing system suddenly became radical and disruptive.

Four decades later he created a comical answer to the naked font with *Eiaculatum*; a naughty sperm alphabet, improvised by hand in a glass workshop. Seminal fluids had first inspired him to make a transparent title for a poster that his assistant at the time, Ruben Steeman, squirted out from a tube of glue. The effect was convincing, as it looked real and enticing. The truly analogue alphabet was born when the provocative self-made designer immortalised these delicate and hand drawn letters in glass. Working with the molten mass was challenging, as many sperms went astray, but in the end the handwriting delivered a wonderful oeuvre arrested in time. With this typeface, Beeke inseminated the world of graphic design with a spontaneous attempt at transparency.

INSEMINATED ILLUSIONS
Anthon Beeke

Eiaculatum, 2009

She once said that the excess produced by the design world was like a propagating infection, since the industry behaves like a proliferating virus, on the verge of becoming a pandemic. Recently, Covid-19 has given another and more profound meaning to 2007's *Crystal Virus* series when artist Pieke Bergmans first captured the act of blowing, pulling and pummelling molten glass; combining it with a piece of furniture, scarring the object in the process, leaving a scorched trail behind. Arrested in time and space, the glass virus and its host espouse one another, becoming inseparable. The burning and deforming of the functional pedestal – be it a table, stool or ladder – is akin to the two-fold transformation inflicted by the coronavirus; a promise of social change for the better after the painful loss of lives and livelihoods.

    Her own life is one of mobility and adventure; she cannot sit still and goes in search of broader horizons and higher goals, constantly challenging herself and her team of experts and craftspeople. She conducts research and produces work, and then travels to undo the stress of business. Born to an artist-mother and a designer-father, the urge to create was in her blood and has motivated her every move; she invests herself in moving house, moving country, moving materials, and moving people with her work. During her journeys to the southern hemispheres of Africa and the Americas, she uses local materials and collaborates with artisans to explore alternative ways of crafting, adding to her repertoire of making skills, taming imperfection into moments of intuitive beauty – almost like natural selection. For Bergmans design is a dialogue between the material and the maker, where the substance's voice is heard and understood by the

Mother of Pearl Meets Crystal Virus, 2008

designer, who at best becomes a translator of energies. This animistic approach where the soul of the material co-designs the object's destiny reaches far into a future where matter will have a right to exist as much as humans.

After studying at four design institutions, Bergmans graduated from the Royal Academy in London but never forgot the first two years of training as a graphic designer in her native Brabant, where her interest for typography was born. This is still visible in her *Phenomeneon* works where she bends and writes with iridescent neon tubes. Heating them to become a malleable material, she then twists, turns and stretches the long shapes of these abstract characters from a yet unknown language. The series plays with light – which in this case is a mercury gas – mysteriously sculpting and distorting the lamps with a random rhythm. She introduces a new fluid vocabulary to a fluorescent lamp, usually known for its stiff rigidity, finding form along the way while controlling the unruly state of the molten glass. Intentionally irrational, her mastering of imperfection only occurs after studying production processes and disruption, liberating the lamp from its industrial origins by art directing it into its ultimate form. The autonomy of materials is what fascinates her and how she, as a designer and artist, can assist the material to coagulate into an even grander and bolder entity.

COAGULATED DIALOGUES
Pieke Bergmans

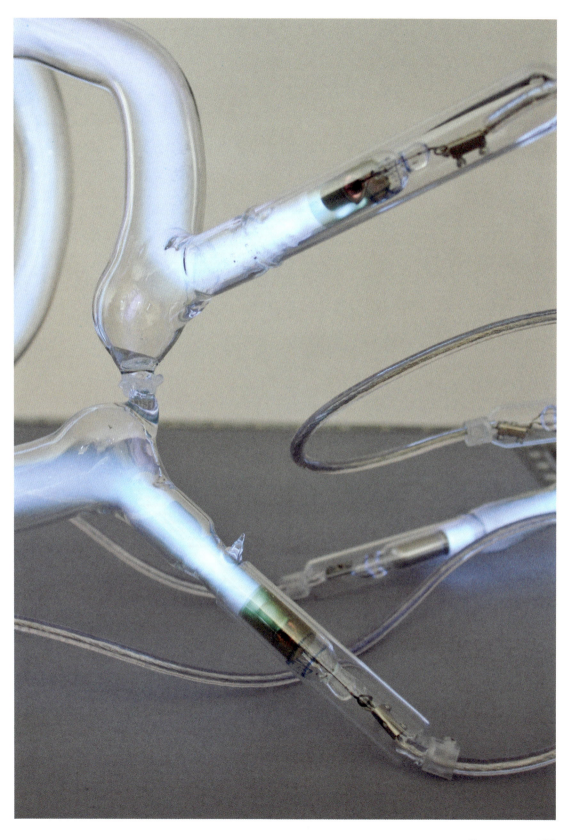
Phenomeneon, 2017

Atelier NL has built up a huge library of hundreds of sand and clay samples gathered over the years. The thorough analysis of these samples, run on every possible scale, from the general landscape to the molecular level, has grown to become a philosophy for the studio's designers Nadine Sterk and Lonny van Ryswyck. Its purpose is to develop projects with aesthetics that emphasize a link between a raw material, its origin and its possible new function. This methodology is applied in various ways, each highlighting several aspects of a same statement.

After several clay projects, Atelier NL applied their methodology to collecting natural sands from Western Europe, following tracks the Romans had left behind. Besides digging sands the designers also archived all kinds of other information: pictures, stones, twigs, geological history and the chemical composition of the samples. Brought together, all this information becomes a material archive.

Back in their studio Atelier NL started to heat the sands, turning them into pieces of glass. The glass industry uses only white, pure sand for the manufacturing of glass, found in a small number of sand quarries around the world. To challenge the conventions of this conservative

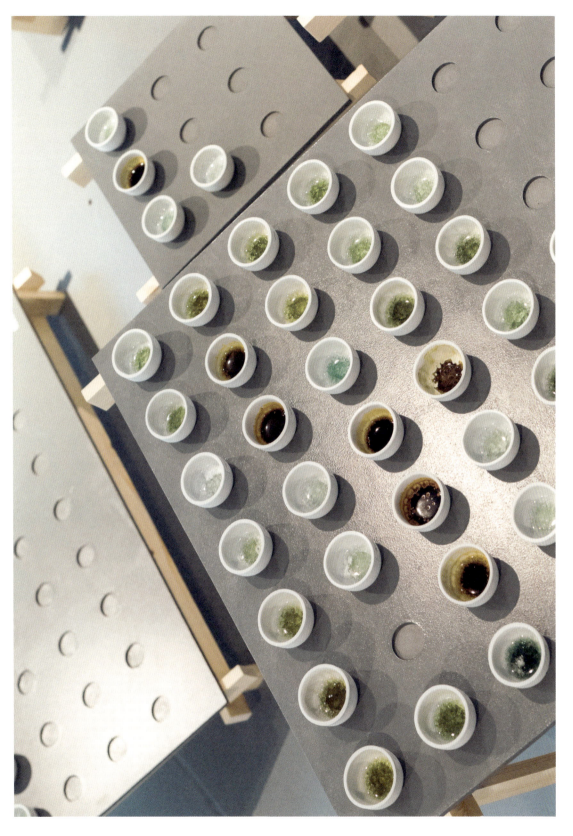

To See the World in a Grain of Sand, 2017–present

industry, Atelier NL is persistently searching and experimenting with local, non-pure sands. Sands from different locations produce not only different colours of glass; melted in the kiln the sands also fracture, foam or harden into crystallization patterns, culminating in 2010's on-going *Sand-Bank* series. Atelier NL strives to uncover the future potential natural wild sands have within them, due to the varied mix of minerals, metals and other components that are attached to the grains.

Atelier NL's projects and products each tell the story of a country or an area; the result brings out the colour spectrum of historical patterns in agriculture and industry. Their work with sand culminated with *To See a World in a Grain of Sand* in 2017, an on-going project that investigates sand as an incredible natural resource by inviting people from all over the world to send them a sample from their favourite location. The sand is then melted into a small glass sample that reveals the unique colours embedded within that very place, and becomes a part of their expanding collaborative archive and touring exhibition.

GLOBAL GLASS
Atelier NL

To See the World in a Grain of Sand, 2017–present

Sand Glass, 2015

The gathering of willow shoots and reeds has been a creative human instinct for millennia, providing a resource for making everything from the first fish traps and baskets to fences, brooms and magic wands. In many communities, the annual reaping was directly linked to local craft traditions, such as in Holland's Biesbosch where the withies were cut. Steven Banken interpreted and honoured this folk custom in *Sheaves*, a rectangular bench comprised either of willow or reeds. Held together by four metal clamps, Banken's minimalist block literally embodies the harvest in a functional piece of design.

The passage of these thin branches through the seasons enchants Banken; organically decaying over time in autumn before becoming compost, unless plucked by a neighbouring bird or animal to build its nest for the winter. This notion of transformation imbues Banken's work, which sometimes uses red iron oxide and tannic acid to stain his pieces in dark blue. From turning wood to hoisting oak beams by using pulleys, Banken's furniture and material experimentations merge his love for craftsmanship with a celebration of workshop production.

AUTUMN HARVEST
Steven Banken

Sheaves, 2009

While flax is still grown in France, Belgium and the Netherlands, it is exported to China to be combed, spun and woven before being reimported to Europe for manufacturing. In her four-year project *l'Ecoucheur*, Pauline Esparon wanted to reclaim the fibre's local identity and its authentic aspects – so often lost in the standardised processing of industrial linen – while also reviving connections to the local craftspeople of Normandy. There, she collaborated with several artisans and suppliers: La Lingère de Saint Martin, providing the scutched flax fibres, Terre de Lin who wove the textiles, Atelier Claudie Burel-Hervé for the upholstery, Entreprise Thibaud Duhamel for the carpentry and Adolphe d'Ennery for the confection of the rug.

Distilling the raw essence of materials comes naturally to Esparon, whose extensive research leads to the finding of form. From investigating the heritage of parchment papermaking to transforming the residue of oil, skin and bones, the rising French star brings a pagan presence to each of her design concepts. In *l'Ecoucheur* totems rise up with layered fringes of flax; the wild fibres dancing when the same application is given to a rug. A monolithic ottoman is composed of compressed felted flax, its natural texture gently breathing like a sleeping beast. A somewhat primal energy pervading Esparon's oeuvre, balanced by a sophisticated aesthetic and neutral colour palettes. Giving autonomous objects animated instincts while simultaneously honouring craftsmanship and regional industries.

OF FORM & THREAD
Pauline Esparon

l'Écoucheur, 2019

l'Écoucheur, 2016

Rattan as an architecture of the body in movement… Elegant, flexible, versatile, gentle to the touch yet hard and resistant are just some of the natural features of this incredible material. Growing amongst the plants and animals of the tropical rainforest, rattan boasts itself as the longest fibre in the world. Aurélie Hoegy rediscovered this magnificent material upon visiting Indonesia, thus enabling her to launch a special design project. Whilst first tracing inspiration from the human body in *The Dancers* in 2016, she now explored the innate liveliness of material itself.

Used in crafts since the dawn of time, rattan has been connected to many styles. Yet one can see how the qualitative and creative potential of the fibre's organic shapes have been relatively constricted through the semi-industrialisation and mass production of its final products. Traditional and practical norms have also played a role in limiting its natural form.

Hoegy's primary focus therefore consisted of drawing upon the material in its essence, along with the idea of forming a symbiosis between bodily movement and the dynamic quality of the fibre. Her object would thus be considered both as a moving body and as a living material, shifting the boundaries from the inert to the living. Doing a residency in Bali gave the artist and designer a most advantageous position, to not only explore the roots and origin of the craft, but also to assimilate the techniques in real time, deepening her sensory knowledge and diving into experimenting with the fibre. Over a one-month stay, she worked in close collaboration with skilful craftsmen in a traditional workshop, completing a full-scale prototype. This first tentative piece started with the classical chair frame. From the legs up, the fibre moulds itself to the skeletal

structure, but as one progresses upwards, the movement unfolds. The stems begin to unbridle themselves and branch out more naturally.

Upon returning to her Paris studio, Hoegy started to fully develop the concept and focused on creating an extensive library of form while immersing herself further into the craft. Additionally she developed a final assembly line starting from traditional techniques and evolving them into the specifics necessary for the final output of this new collection.

Rattan fibres need to pass many stages of processing before they are ready to use. After harvest, the spiny leaf sheaths are removed on the spot. Rattan that is small in diameter is then subjected to a process called *runti* or *lunti* in Indonesian, which means removing the siliceous epidermis by various methods; rubbing, fumigation, oil curing, bleaching, washing, polishing… These treatments are necessary to avoid defects and to increase processing possibilities and the market value. Following a path of experimentation and listening to the fibre, Hoegy was able to make three prototypes whose movement marries the traditional structure of the chairs while keeping the rattan's own organic forms. This gives a natural and fluid anchorage to the furniture. Within the changing context of an increasingly virtual and disconnected society, Hoegy believes we need to reconnect with materials. Design can become a powerful rebalancing tool through archetypical objects; creating a collaborative symbiosis between the object, the body and the environment.

WILD THINGS
Aurélie Hoegy

Meeting Points, 2019

Meeting Points is a working prototype for a reconfigurable composite material system; a tensility and equilibrium of wood and fibre, only made possible through each individual connection and the intuitive hands that created them. These different meeting points – between fibre and structure, material and space – arise in response to the design processes of the Bedouin tent-making craft. A porous self-structuring tapestry; at both the scale of its dynamic lattice structure and the pliable hand-knitted geometric pattern, lending the material system its mechanical properties. Evolving through collaboration, it seeks to sustain traditional design processes, passed down from generation to generation.

Through the communal efforts of 58 rural and Bedouin community members from various governorates across Jordan (40 of which were women), the first iteration has already helped foster new opportunities for individuals to contribute to and benefit from the social, cultural and economic development in their respective communities. The future advancement of *Meeting Points* will be based on the development of innovative structural fabric prototypes within these social systems, with various potential architectural applications both in Jordan and beyond.

Meeting Points, 2019

Matters of Time film stills, 2019

The Bedouin tent or Beit-al-Shaar has been the subject of much reverence for its beauty and for the poetry of its construction; a process that has evolved through a continuing heritage and the activity of women. Yet the legacies of its cumulative and communal design ingenuity continue to be disregarded within the contemporary catalogue of design knowledge in Jordan, and are instead marginalized as architectures without architects. A product of a humanised process, the Bedouin tent is a responsive archetype and performative architecture that should be attributed to the lineage of women who have communally engineered it. *Meeting Points* therefore establishes an understanding of architecture as a process rather than as a purely material outcome; the formulation of an adaptable creative-cultural form that explores the meeting points between material and structure, between nature and designed space, and between designer and community.

WOVEN ARCHITECTURE
Abeer Seikaly

The idea that we could farm patterns in soil once seemed to be a fantasy, yet as designers study the links between bio-technology, agriculture and design, a new domain of sustainable materials emerges. In that sphere, Diana Scherer's award-winning work is poetically positioned; she collaborated with biologists and ecologists from the Radboud University in Nijmegen before designing 3D printed subterranean template structures on which to grow – and harvest – root systems.

Wheat is her yarn and provides a fast-growing solution, morphing its small stems into romantic lacelike weaves. Wheat is a millennial material, a grass grown for its grain that has sustained civilization for over 11,000 years. The fibre's strength is evidenced by the straw that covered thatched roofs from the Bronze Age until the late 19th century. Since wheat is cultivated on more land area than any other crop, there is also an opportunity to mix the production of materials with the rearing of our greatest food source.

Scherer is fascinated by how the root system of a plant is in fact its brain, citing Charles Darwin as the first to watch the behaviour of plant roots: "In his book *The Power of Movements of Plants*, he describes how roots do not passively grow down, but move and observe. A root navigates, knows what's up and down, observes gravity and localizes moisture and chemicals. Darwin discovered that plants are a

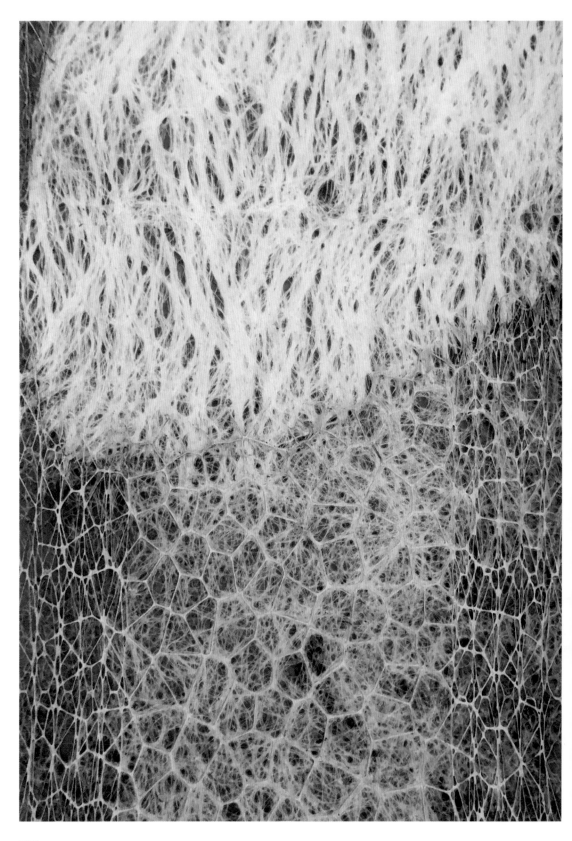

Interwoven #32, 2016

lot more intelligent than everybody thought. For contemporary botanists, this buried matter is still a wondrous land. There is a global investigation to discover this hidden world. I also want to explore it and apply the intelligence of plants in my work."

Scherer's designs are inspired by the shapes of nature itself – geometric structures, snowflakes and shells. The artist's intervention is double sided: sometimes she directs the roots' movements, other times she allows them to run their course. Once the material has reached the desired design, the crop is reaped, revealing an underworld of swirls and grids that are as intricate as the finest oriental embroidery, delicate paper cut or lavish Arabian lattice.

Her conceptual works preview a time when such braids will be ecologically produced matter, when our objects and garments might be conceived, grown and gathered. With the benefits of energy-efficient production and the ability to store greenhouse gasses, the project is being developed further; new plants are being experimented with, and multiple applications are just around the corner, allowing us to dream up an entirely biological landscape for fashion and design alike.

ORGANIC LACE
Diana Scherer

Hyper Rhizome #5, 2020

Interwoven, 2017

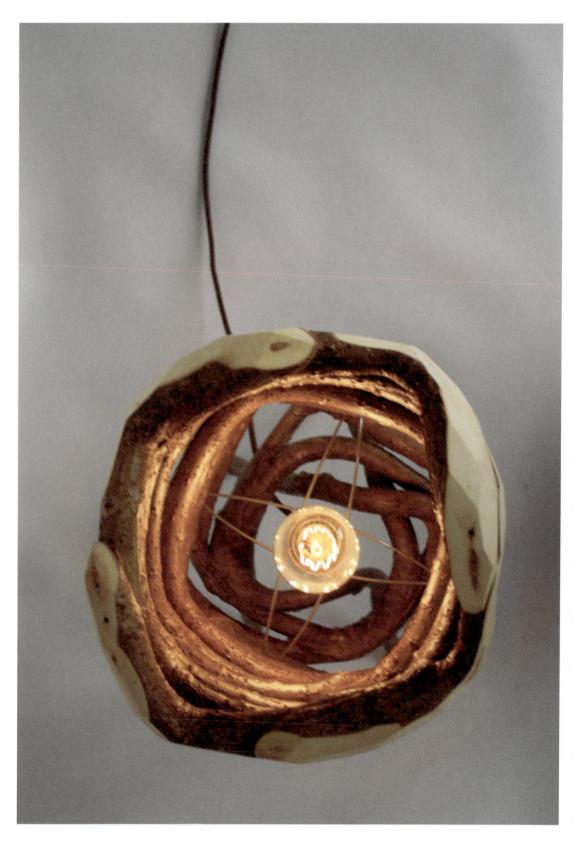

Edwardes Chair, 2012–2018

Lumsdale Table Lamp, 2012-2018

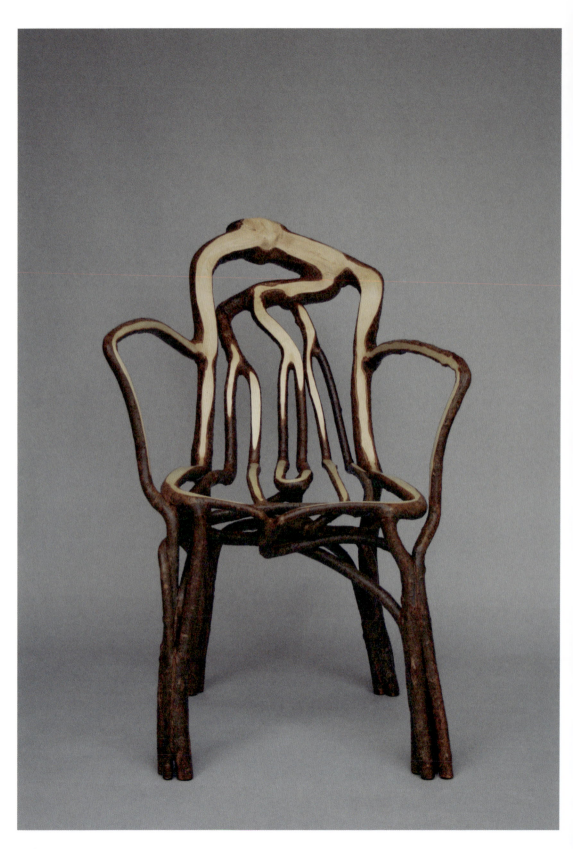

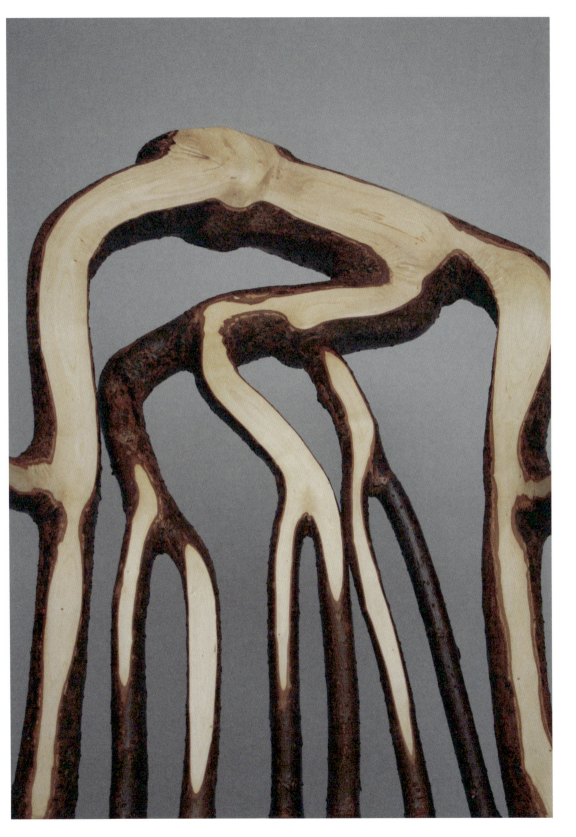

Gatti Chair, 2012-2018

An incredible sense of wonder and anticipation permeates when travelling through the English countryside to Derbyshire. Something incredible is about to be revealed, and one cannot wait for the surprise. The future becomes reality when walking through specialised orchards to observe the astonishing trees; and literally witness design burgeoning in their branches. Slowly maturing into their functional shapes and waiting to be harvested – to be used as a chair, a table or a lamp once they are perfected.

The promise of bio-engineered production finally comes into focus, even if these designs by nature are crafted prototypes, and for now, a germinating prospect. Some sensational pieces take seven years to grow, with a tender human hand guiding them, helping the tree to sketch out an ever better model. These pieces are one-of-a-kind and unique in their expression, now sought after by cultural institutions around the world.

Some chairs appear like a bunch of endearing twigs, hovering on fragile legs, while others are majestic and robust, built to command presence in any imposing interior. The forms cannot be controlled and live out their lives influenced by the age, character and quality of each tree. They can be springy and resilient, or malleable and pliant; the tree's intuitive intelligence decides what form can be best rooted during the growing process.

These astounding proceedings open up the possibilities of serial products that are curated to find form in the nursery of biological knowledge. And it is human curiosity and empathy for our environment that brings these prospects further, a possible form of design farming.

As a designer and artisan, Gavin Munro previewed his career in childhood when an overgrown bonsai reminded him of a chair, triggering the naive dream that one could possibly grow furniture. After studying art and design, he came closer to his vision when becoming an apprentice to a traditional cabinetmaker. Building barns in Britain and eco-houses in California further connected him to trees, logs and planks, yet it was while carefully constructing – and almost healing – driftwood furniture that he understood how design should be grown from scratch, skipping the manufacturing process and other wasteful stages. Of course, outsider folk art grown from willow was an initial inspiration yet in his work, Munro perfected the technique and used wood from various trees. With great patience and dedication, he and Alice Munro take care of their open-air atelier at Full Grown, lending a helping hand whenever needed to streamline growth; also imagining new product ideas and reaching out to new markets. The couple handles the subject matter with great care, cherishing the connection with their growing botanical friends. Respect is the recipe for a relationship that is mature and mutual, giving the forces of cultivation the best chance to become masterworks.

PATIENCE IS A VIRTUE
Full Grown

a freshly harvested Gatti Chair

It was Martim Affonso that, in 1532, brought the first sugar cane seedling to Brazil. However it was not until 2016 that Rodrigo Ambrosio transformed it into furniture. These cane reeds produce a honey without bees that can be converted into fuel, sugar, syrup and spirits – and now, into design.

The *Engenho* or *Sugar Chair* carries with it the ambiguity of form and function, as well as that of Brazil's own cultural and economic history. During the colonial period, sugar was one of the most prized products in Europe and, due to its high price, was only consumed by the elite. Colonial expansion abroad lead to the Sugarcane Cycle in Brazil, which generated twice the nation's income attained from gold. However, this important crop is also stained by a heritage of inequality and injustice for the indigenous and African people that worked as slaves, and bitter memories of a patriarchal society in the hands of mill owners.

In his creation, Ambrosio ground, boiled, moulded and dried Brazil's historic resource; looking at sugar in a new light. A passionate expression for his country's culture, uniting design and gastronomy to produce a piece that synthetizes the sweet challenge of being Brazilian today. To be appreciated bit by bit, like the pieces of molasses left in the refrigerator by Ambrosio's mother, consumed on hot days in Alagoas.

SUGAR MAN
Rodrigo Ambrosio

Sugar Chair, 2016

wooden mould for Sugar Chair, 2016

When thinking about their children's future and the state of the planet, many designers are conscious of our depleting resources. Stone, minerals and gems are usually extracted from the earth, before being manufactured into shape. But what if this process could be reversed and we could grow three-dimensional stone objects without the need for mining? That was the basis of Laura Lynn Jansen's and Thomas Vailly's research project *CaCO3*, otherwise known as calcium carbonate. The couple collaborated with scientists, geologists and craftspeople to investigate this exciting possibility.

The collection of tabletop objects starts with a thin nylon structure that has been 3D printed before it is deposited for a period of weeks in thermo-mineral caves that have been specifically chosen because of their high calcium content. Discovered on a trip to the Auvergne in France, the stalactite grottos are found near springs where hot water surfaces, rich in minerals after travelling through volcanic fissures in the earth. The resulting limestone rapidly attaches itself to the vase and plate skeletons, filling in the blanks like a chubby calc lace. "We did not approach this project with the idea of having full control of the end product," remarks Vailly, "what interested us was the idea of designing the embryo of a stone object and then letting a natural process take over." The items are respectfully priced based on their weight and the number of days needed for petrification. Part fossil, part future, the cultivated material is strong and akin to terracotta or porcelain. It previews a time when stone can be grown in union with nature. Design as an additive rather than subtractive force.

THE EMBRYO OF STONE
Laura Lynn Jansen & Thomas Vailly

Care for Milk, 2016

Giving value to materials is a goal common to many contemporary designers. They explore the intrinsic qualities of each ingredient and remind us of their worth, especially when forgotten in our fast-paced digital lives. The milk industry is one example of how a former staple in daily life can be negatively impacted over time, with plummeting sales, devaluation, mass industrialisation and competition from dairy alternatives. Ekaterina Semenova decided to explore how milk could be honoured again, seen through the sepia-shaded lens of her earthenware.

Care for Milk is a collection of biscuit pottery that is dipped in milk before turning velvet tones of auburn after further firing. During her research, Semenova experimented with different dairy products and discovered that hues would vary depending on fat content. She also witnessed the liquid's remarkable effectiveness in waterproofing and durability. Conscious not to be wasteful, milk was sourced as donated leftovers collected in local Dutch neighbourhoods. The simple rounded shapes of the ceramics celebrate the wholesome experience of enjoying milk in a cup or bowl – as if beholding it – with thick accompanying plates that elevate these vessels on a pedestal. This method of growing natural colour as a sealant shows how food refuse can become a respected resource, transformed into an aesthetic medium to alert the public about pertinent sustainability issues and related socio-cultural causes.

CULTIVATING COLOUR
Ekaterina Semenova

A new generation of designers are becoming investigative; delving deep into the inconvenient truths of unsustainable production while often uncovering surprising making techniques in the process. They simultaneously generate research, materials and form with the potential to shift manufacturing in the right direction after decades of environmental ignorance and abuse. To shed light on this notion, Agne Kucerenkaite is a designer who is not afraid to get her hands dirty; literally. She transforms pollution into an alternative source of colour, growing beauty out of society's mess. The Lithuanian has been studying how non-toxic metals and plant-based refuse can be applied to ceramics, glass and textiles. Where others do not, Kucerenkaite sees value and delight in waste.

Ignorance is Bliss: Tableware, 2016

In *Ignorance is Bliss*, she has created a rich natural palette of orange, red, brown and black, by mixing factory metal waste into porcelain clay and glaze. The by-products were gathered in soil from a remediation plant, a zinc factory and drinking water purification companies in the Netherlands. This method gives unique vivid shades to tiles and a collection of elegant tabletop. She has also applied these powdered hues to textiles, when the iron sludge from a drinking water supplier becomes dyes for cotton and wool yarns, woven into table runners and handmade rugs. Other waste is sourced in the food, beverage, cosmetic and pharmaceutical sectors. Ironically, iron also becomes a mordant in the project, ensuring the colours stay for generations to come.

NURTURING WASTE
Agne Kurcerenkaite

The tension between the organic and the manmade, between natural and the artificial, is perhaps most laid bare whenever an object breaks. Part casualty, part road kill, the leftover elements are imbued with memories from their former use. Yet what happens when these elements are resuscitated and instilled with a new raison d'être? From *Kintsugi*, the 15th century Japanese tradition of golden joinery on pottery, to the recycling of waste materials so prominent in design today, history has shown how there's beauty in decay and power in rebirth.

By applying a salt-based chemical solution to shattered ceramic vases, Lukas Wegwerth was able to cultivate crystals as a multifaceted vector for repair; breathing new life and energy into otherwise discarded objects. Over the course of 4 to 21 days – or even left in the studio for up to two years – the uncontrollable crystalline formations become like viruses, taking over their host's shape in molecular magic. This is orchestrated in a mineral matter that is traditionally known to emit its own spirit – a transformative second layer of soul embedded within the vase's essence. This form of growing design can produce different crystal hues depending on the types of salts Wegwerth employs, from opaque whites and translucent pinks to muddled shades of lavender and purple. Letting nature and chance add a spiritual tint to these contemporary amulets.

REPAIRED BY CRYSTAL
Lukas Wegwerth

Crystallisation 79, 2016

Crystallisation 92, 2016

The design sector has been slow to address the use of animal products in manufacturing. The leather, fur and natural fibre industries are notorious, but beyond these materials countless other products include animal-based oils and ingredients, from brushes and tapes to most plastics and industrial glues. With animals increasingly acknowledged as sentient beings by governments around the world, and growing public knowledge about the cruelty that surrounds livestock farming, it is time for the design community to grow a conscience and evolve new solutions.

Vegan design is the term coined to describe Erez Nevi Pana's practice. He feels that choosing awareness leads to action, which in turn can expand this important discussion. After personal introspection about his own diet and consumption, he realised that by extension his design concepts also should strive to be guilt-free. The questions he raises are multiple and pertinent: How long will we continue to sponsor practices with which most of us don't associate in our own daily actions? What would be the substitutes for animal ingredients in sanding paper, glue, wood wax and paints to accomplish the design of a vegan wooden chair? Is it possible to reach a level of purity and virtue in a 100% animal-free vegan design?

Following studies and travel in India, Nevi Pana gained a deeper understanding of *Ahimsā*, the ancient principle of nonviolence towards all living things. While standardised silk production involves the boiling of live silkworms in their cocoons, in *Unravelled*,

Overall, 2016, in collaboration with Ines Bressand

Lot's Wife, 2015

the designer meticulously undid the fibres after the worms had vacated their metamorphosis chambers; combining them with straw fragments from the baskets used in unethical silk cultivation to weave an animated highly-textural textile.

Growing organic matter is also a way Nevi Pana draws our attention to environmentalism; from fermenting soil and fungi – a sustainable mixture which expands overnight before it is baked into moulded object – to the plight of the fragile Dead Sea which sees more than 20 million tonnes of salt sink to its depths annually, a by-product of the nearby potash industry. The resulting devastation includes both flooding and lowered water levels, as well as desertification and vast quantities of sinkholes. For *Bleached*, he attaches loofa gourds to wooden stool frames made from carpentry discards, before immersing the structures in the salty body of water, absorbing the crystalline minerals over a period of months – extracting and expanding form at the same time. This research into the Dead Sea and salt started during his studies at the Design Academy Eindhoven where he created gleaming white tiles and encrusted clay vessels. To paraphrase Jane Goodall, one could say that Nevi Pana walked into the desert a designer and came out as an activist.

A NEW CONSCIENCE
Erez Nevi Pana

Unravelled, 2018

Bleached, 2016

One of the greatest challenges in the recycling of fashion relates to the fibre content in blended yarns; these garments often end up in landfill or are destroyed using chemicals. Often labels are inaccurate and misleading and sorting is a time-consuming process. Chiara Tommencioni Pisapia has been thinking outside the box while investigating a surprising solution that has been fluttering right under our nose the whole time: moths. By inviting them to break down the natural fibres in clothing waste, she hopes to activate the circular process; an urgent and colossal issue in an industry widely regarded as the second most polluting on the planet.

The Central Saint Martins Material Futures graduate sees the insects as potential partners and has designed a miniature farm to illustrate her theory. By decomposing yarns with their enzymes, cloth moths are able to absorb the vast majority of blended fabrics; their infamous taste for keratin-rich wools and silk used instead as a positive force. After digesting the material, a dust-like bio-residue is produced, able to be transformed into biodegradable objects, thus giving the source fibres a second life. As part of her research, Tommencioni Pisapia collaborated with scientists at the University of York to explore how the larvae enzymes could one day create an amino acid capable of recycling textile waste on a larger scale. This journey continues, reflecting the Italian designer's dedication to sustainable solutions and a broader future when biology, nature and design will merge.

MADE BY MOTHS
Chiara Tommencioni Pisapia

Made by Moths, 2019

Made by Moths, 2019

True innovation tantalizes and propels the fashion industry into exciting new territories. Unlocking with each step a new level of design freedom in terms of geometry, material physicality, scale, colour and transparency. Stratasys is one such pioneer that has been pushing the boundaries of fashion and technology. 2019 marked a pivotal point when the studio was able to achieve dimensional printing onto textiles for the first time. The intricate scales and the deeper architectural structure are capable of manipulating the absorption of light, much like existing – yet unsustainable – sequins. Thus the skill and vision of the singular, unique craftsman can once again become anchored into the heart of the production process since 3D technologies can act as a direct continuation of the artist's hand.

For spring / summer 2020, the fashion trio ThreeASFOUR utilised this new printing technology in a couture dress that explores the microscopic venation of butterfly wings, especially the insect's colouration when fluttering in light. Named after the Greta Oto (the glass-winged butterfly), the design plays with light and colour to produce a lenticular

Human Plant, spring / summer 2020

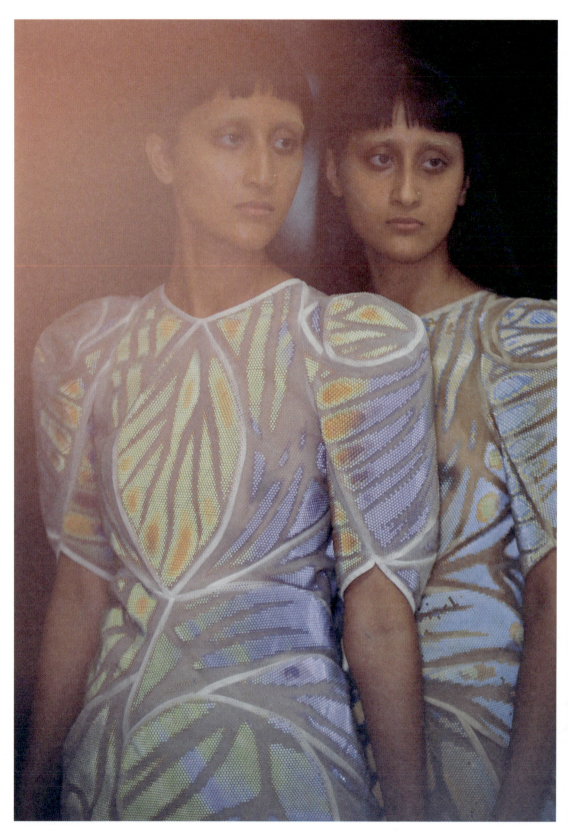

Human Plant, spring / summer 2020

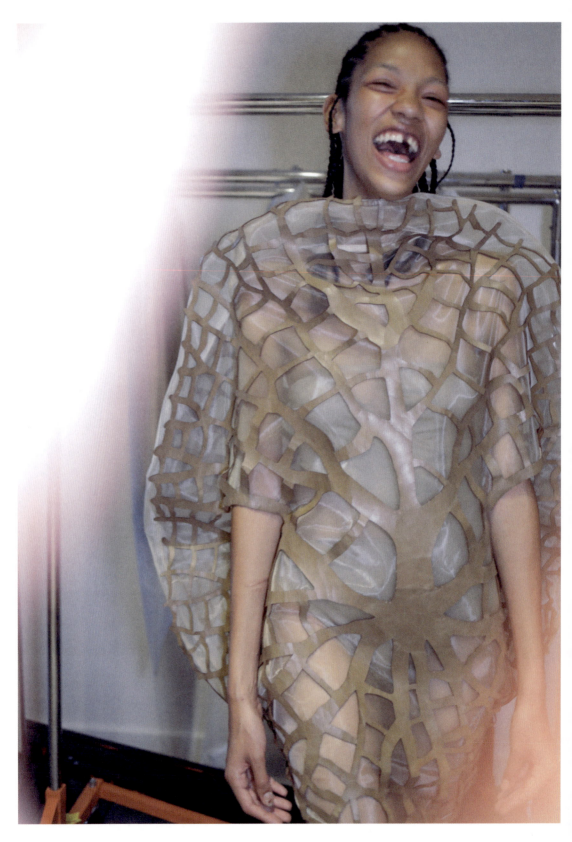

effect: by printing spherical, fishscale-sized cells onto the fabric that consist of a clear lens, with two strips of colour underlying them; the colour of the dress shifts with each diminutive change of angle in illumination, creating an iridescent and mesmerising display of golden-blue hues.

The dress is part of a collection called *Human Plant* which articulates the life force found both in people and the natural world. The organic formations of plants create sculptural garment shapes while the sacred geometry of leaves inspires veined motifs and shades taken from nature's neutral hues. As the designers so poetically state when describing their biological inspiration, "Plants transmute light into life. Human beings transmute life into consciousness and love. These three – light, life, and love – are one, each an expression of the other, three dimensions of the same existence. Unity is the basis of all existence, unity of life is the unity of consciousness."

A FASHION (R)EVOLUTION
threeASFOUR

Jonathan Chapman, Professor and Director of Doctoral Studies at Carnegie Mellon University's School of Design, once said we should create objects that still have something to tell us: "Products must mutually evolve alongside users, sustaining value by revealing their true beauty only through the slow passing of time… Modern products seriously lack character and allure; they are too smart and precise, removing all possible surprise, mystery and, perhaps above all, the process of engaging with them."

Inspired by this reflection, Violaine Buet followed a winding trail all the way to a natural and living material: seaweed. Given the wealth of discoveries and promises of this material, she started to tame macroalgae, like a true craftswoman of the material, using kelp harvested on the beaches of her native Brittany. Buet's seaweed has allowed her to weave, tuft, dye, engrave, cut out, braid, emboss, knot, print, observe, caress and contemplate.

This process of exploration gave birth to new textiles, the material itself also helping the designer invent new processes. And like

kelp textile samples

with a birth of any kind, this is accompanied by a multitude of questions – about techniques, applications, identity, aesthetics, rhythm, systems, and more broadly, about the ecosystem at large. Which new combinations and structures can be developed to magnify this material, as well as the weaving process itself? The palette of possibilities that has opened up is vast.

Working with a natural resource that is not yet coveted is almost like raising a tidal wave: the gap between the small, intuitive gesture of weaving this unruly marine plant and the potentially devastating impact on marine life is troubling. Buet sees how a great interest in kelp biomaterials could develop very fast; yet she hopes that this new relationship between algae and humans will instead take on a slower pace, not looking for quick results and profits but for good on the long term. A renewal of our relationship with nature, along the lines of a great mesological reflection.

SEA WEAVE
Violaine Buet

kelp textile sample

kelp textile samples

Cocoon Cabinet #5, 2017

Having grown up as the daughter of a beekeeper in the French Alps, Marlène Huissoud's destiny was written early on. As a designer, she has pushed the boundaries of where insects can take materials, innovating new applications while previewing a time when bio-design can promise sustainable and ethical solutions. While conducting a Material Futures Masters at Central Saint Martins in 2014, she started to work with insects, varnishing layers of paper with the natural Serisin glue found in silk yarns, thus creating a wood-like bio-leather. She also treated bees' propolis like glass, blowing a collection of tall and fragrant vases that resemble vertical logs. To make the darkly lacquered vases, she first went to work in a glass workshop to unveil the synergies that could be formulated between her apiary resource and traditional blowing methods. Forged at 100 degrees centigrade, instead of the usual 1200 used for glass, these towering totems are also finished using glass-engraving techniques on the surface.

The small and round shapes of the silkworm cocoons have continued to inspire form throughout Huissoud's career in the art-design domain, exploring a sculptural vocabulary that is entirely organic. In *Cocoon*, she covered a cabinet with thousands of the bubble shells before coating them with a shiny honeybee bio-resin. As a conscious designer, Huissoud only uses cocoons that have been vacated by the moths. More recently, she has taken to the lost cocoon process of casting metal sculptures, or building cavernous clay homes to welcome insects back to our gardens and rooftops. With 40% of insect species declining – one third of which are endangered – our relationship with them as a design partner is therefore delicate. We must tread lightly and learn from insects, restoring balance in the fragile environment we share.

FROM INSECTS
Marlène Huissoud

From Insects, 2014

Man and machine are often able to create beauty from humble means, and the recent focus on extrusion in design is a technique that is gaining momentum. Jólan van der Wiel uses magnetism to stretch materials into otherworldly forms – such as stools, candleholders, garments and even footwear. He has built several *Gravity Tools* to literally grow materials that flow somewhere between surface, sculpture and architecture. The machines are an extension of van der Wiel's hands, using liquid resins infused with iron powder to craft spikey textures. Powerful magnets are lowered above a warmed two-compound paste, and when raised slowly, the organic structures emerge before hardening in the cool air. The effect is mesmerising; a so-called dragonstone that looks like a futuristic stalagmite.

Van der Wiel has collaborated with Iris van Herpen on several occasions, culminating in the *Magnetic Moon Dress* in the couturier's autumn / winter 2013–14 collection. Despite its sharp appearance, the dress is actually supple like a regular textile. This lunar landscape is just one of the many worlds created by van der Wiel. Dimensions are no barrier either; he has recently completed a full-size *Monster Table* with the assistance of the Goudsmit Magnetics Group.

MAGNETIC FORCES
Jólan van der Wiel

the Growing Pavilion at Dutch Design Week, 2019

the Growing Pavilion at Dutch Design Week, 2019

Their name encapsulates their actions since Company New Heroes is indeed about local and social heroes; pushing human and ecological progress with conviction and dedication. Their story does not follow the normal design itinerary; they don't even come from a formal design background but are instead a collective of writers, thinkers, image-makers and stage artists that sample and narrate new ways of living and conceiving, designing strategies instead of products. They combine performance with audiovisual arts and invade all aspects of culture, working on connecting people with themselves and others. Under the creative genius of its founder Lucas de Man, they come together to complement one another and undertake social challenges as a group. One of the members, the architect Pascal Leboucq, initiated a project when he became interested in mycelium as a building material. He connected with Eric Klarenbeek, a designer that had already experimented with the mushrooming matter.

Stimulated and motivated, the two creatives took on a full-scale architectural challenge: to build a pavilion that is completely ecological in its components, from the biomaterial structure to all the bio-objects it contains. A sustainable vision unfolds as one enters the space where everything is conceived; from plants, trees and agricultural remnants to the reed floor, mycelium walls and timber structure. The display includes a chair made from compressed flax, a dress grown from roots, goblets manufactured from seaweed – suddenly the future is here, and one witnesses how society can be made without waste. The growing of this material will lead to harvests that are only just beginning; not yet noticed by large building corporations that continue to erect glass towers. However, sometime in the next decade, further research will bear fruit and blossom into an alternative, often indigenous, industry where ancient methodologies will be rekindled and adapted to contemporary demands.

The *Growing Pavilion* is a round temporary design space constructed from mushroom mycelium, which is grown and harvested from hay bales at the entrance. This cultural circus provides a magnificent preview of tomorrow and the materialization that will evolve. The liquid in the roots of the mushrooms provides the strength in the mycelium that can last for decades. The matter is further stabilized with a bio-based coating that was first developed by the Inca people; indeed, indigenous cultures hold a multitude of secret recipes that can help us build and design. The mushrooming material grows at a rapid pace and promises a multitude of possibilities for industrial production. It is organic and malleable, able to be easily moulded into shape, inviting design to consider its potential function. Compressed into panels, the mycelium is mounted onto a wooden frame and is therefore flexible and recyclable. The solid floor is pressed from sturdy reed that is still visible on the surface, doubling as an eco-print, and surrounding a pond with actual cattails to understand the intimacy of the processes on show. Here nature and human nature are connected.

GROWING PAVILION
Company New Heroes

the Growing Pavilion at Dutch Design Week, 2019

One is a double Virgo, the other a double Pisces, and they double as creative partners and design directors, as well as curators in art, design and fashion. They have shared twenty years together, made up of travel, discovery, culture and inspiration, and have inspired others with ideas for trends, exhibitions and books. They think differently and the same, often completing each other's sentences, their genetic codes balancing masculine and feminine energy.

Lidewij Edelkoort is a renowned forecaster of anthropological and cultural change. Philip Fimmano is an observer of societal codes of conduct. She also dedicated herself to education by becoming chairwoman of the Design Academy of Eindhoven, and later founding the School of Form in Poland and scripting a textile masters at the New School in New York. He followed suit by mentoring forecasting students at Polimoda in Florence.

As curators, they have a solid record of exhibitions staged internationally – from Japan to South Africa, Israel, Italy, France, Sweden, Norway, Russia, Belgium, the Netherlands and the United States – on topics that translate the major currents of our time, such as Post-Fossil, Earth Matters, Talking Textiles and Fetishism in Fashion. In this brick-thick publication, they have assembled a roster of designers that preview a future of responsible making, circular thinking, ethical practice and aesthetics. They therefore believe this book is a testimony to the future.

THE AUTHORS
Lidewij Edelkoort
& Philip Fimmano

Texts

All texts by Lidewij Edelkoort & Philip Fimmano, with additional transcripts by:

page 114, June Yoon
page 342, Angelique Spaninks
page 356, Aurélie Hoegy
page 362, Abeer Seikaly
page 422, Violaine Buet

Designer Index

About A Worker, pages 64–73
Rodrigo Ambrosio, pages 386–389
Anton Alvarez, pages 138–143
Atelier NL, pages 342–349
Marjan van Aubel & James Shaw, pages 28, 242–245
Steven Banken, pages 350–351
Anthon Beeke, pages 334–337
Pieke Bergmans, pages 44, 338–341
Violaine Buet, pages 55, 422–427
Nacho Carbonell, pages 300–303
Paul Cocksedge, pages 32, 224–231
Company New Heroes, pages 434–441
Piet Hein Eek, pages 170–177
Pauline Esparon, pages 48, 352–355
Full Grown, pages 376–385
Femke van Gemert, pages 116–119
Daniel Harris, pages 120–127
Paul Heijnen, pages 168–169
Olivier van Herpt & Sander Wassink, pages 276–281
Pepe Heykoop, pages 144–149
Aurélie Hoegy, pages 356–359
Dick van Hoff, pages 56, 62–63
Beer Holthuis, pages 262–265
Marlène Huissoud, pages 428–431
Laura Lynn Jansen & Thomas Vailly, pages 390–391
Dirk Vander Kooij, pages 150–151
Agne Kurcerenkaite, pages 396–399
Eilssa Lacoste, pages 266–271
Martin Laforet, pages 216–223
Max Lamb, pages 188–199
Kostas Lambridis, pages 158–167
Sun Lee, pages 112–115
Tomáš Libertíny, pages 310–313
Carlo Lorenzetti, pages 294–299
Liuxu Luo, pages 128–133
Peter Marigold, pages 178–181
Matter Design/MIT, pages 204–209
Erez Nevi Pana, pages 404–411
Yuko Nishikawa, pages 272–275
Taeg Nishimoto, pages 252–255
Sho Ota, pages 182–187
People from the Porcelain Factory, pages 82–89
Simone Post, pages 134–136
Lex Pott, pages 200–203
Zoe Joe Rae, pages 232–241
Gianmaria della Ratta, pages 256–261

Rutger de Regt, pages 322–323
Peter Salera, pages 152–157
Diana Scherer, pages 52, 368–375
Abeer Seikaly, pages 360–367
Ekaterina Semenova, pages 392–395
Social Label, pages 90–97
Roland Pieter Smit, pages 98–101
Ben Storms, pages 210–215
Studio Job, pages 58–61
Salem van der Swaagh, pages 108–111
ThreeASFOUR, pages 416–421
Bas Timmer, pages 74–81
Chiara Tommencioni Pisapia, pages 412–415
Arnout Visser, pages 328–333
Jeroen Wand, pages 36, 282–287
Waste No More, pages 102–107
Philipp Weber, pages 324–327
Lukas Wegwerth, pages 400–403
Jólan van der Wiel, pages 432–433
Debbie Wijskamp, pages 246–251
Jorien Wiltenburg, pages 314–317
Floris Wubben, pages 288–293
Hongjie Yang, pages 304–309
Oskar Zieta, pages 43, 318–321

Images

All images courtesy of the following designers & photographers:

page 6, photography by Daniel Costa, creation & styling by Sergio Machado

pages 8, 11–12, 15–16, 19–20, 23–24, 27–28, 31, 35, 39–40, 43–44, 47, 51, 59, 61 top, photography & styling by Juliette Chrétien & Daniel Costa

pages 32, 226–228, 230–231, Mark Cocksedge courtesy Friedman Benda Gallery

pages 36, 282, 284–285, 287, courtesy Studio Jeroen Wand

pages 48, 353–355, Stéphane Ruchaud

pages 52, 368, 370–371, 373–375, Diana Scherer

pages 55, 423, 425–427, Violaine Buet

page 61 bottom, Arjan Benning

pages 56, 63, Petra Janssen, Studio Boot

pages 64–65, Marie Taillefer

pages 67, 73, Loan Lamoureux

page 68, Bobby So

pages 70–71, About a Worker

pages 75–80, Tony Dočekal, courtesy Sheltersuit

pages 82–84, 86–87, 89, Arkadiusz Szwed

pages 90, 93, 95, Petra Janssen

pages 91, 96, Luuk van Loon, Studio Boot

page 99, Femke Rijerman

pages 100–101, Rene van der Hulst

pages 109–111, Ilco Kemmere

pages 112, 115, Shen Yichen

page 116, Leo Veger

pages 118–119, Femke van Gemert

pages 121–123, 125–127, London Cloth Company

pages 129–133, Liuxu Luo

pages 134–136, Studio Simone Post

pages 139–141, Sasa Stucin

page 143, Gustav Almestål

pages 144–145, 147–149, Annemarijne Bax

page 151, Studio Dirk Vander Kooij

pages 152, 154–155, 157, Peter Salera

pages 159–160, 162–167, 217–223, Jean-Pierre Vaillancourt, courtesy Carpenters Workshop Gallery

pages 169, 276, 278–279, 281, 304–307, 309, 392–394, Ronald Smits

pages 170–171, 173–174, 176–177, courtesy Studio Piet Hein Eek

pages 179–181, Anna Arca, courtesy Sarah Myerscought Gallery

pages 182–183–187, Sho Ota

pages 188–193, 195, Angus Mil, courtesy Gallery FUMI

pages 196, 198–199, courtesy Salon 94 Design

pages 201–202, Lex Pott

pages 205–209, courtesy Mediated Matter / MIT & Quarra Stone

pages 210–212, 214–215, Alexander Popelier

pages 233–236, 238–241, Mustafa Sami & Karen Gager

pages 242, 244–245, Petr Krejci

pages 246–248, 251, Debbie Wijskamp

page 250, courtesy Serax

pages 252–253, 255, TN/MOS

pages 256–258, 260, Gianmaria della Ratta

pages 261–262, Iris Rijskamp, courtesy Design Academy Eindhoven

pages 264–265, Beer Holthuis

pages 266, 270–271, Ties Bemelmans, courtesy Everyday Gallery

page 267, Erika Emerén

page 269, Antoine Maillier

pages 273–275, Yuko Nishikawa

pages 288–292, Studio Floris Wubben

page 295, Carlo Lorenzetti

pages 296–297, 299, Ronald Smits & Dutch Invertuals

pages 301, 303, Marco Moretto, courtesy NODUS by Il Piccolo Srl

pages 310–311, 313, Margaux Nieto

pages 314–316, Jorien Wiltenburg

page 319, Rutger de Regt

pages 320–321, 323, Studio Zieta

pages 325–327, Philipp Weber

pages 328–329, 333, Arthur Rotier

page 330, Marthe Visser